Rhetorical Devices:
A HANDBOOK AND ACTIVITIES FOR STUDENT WRITERS

Prestwick House

Rhetorical
Devices:
A HANDBOOK AND ACTIVITIES FOR STUDENT WRITERS

Senior Editor:
Paul Moliken

Editor:
Douglas Grudzina

Writer:
Brendan McGuigan

Reviewing Teachers:
Sharon M. Ammon, English Department Chair
Memorial High School, Houston, TX

Kathleen Carr

Peter Glaser

Cover and Text Design:
Jen Mendoza

Layout and Production:
Jerry Clark

Prestwick House

© 2007 Copyrighted by Prestwick House, Inc.

Printed in the United States of America.

Revised December, 2011.

ISBN: 978-158049-766-4

TABLE OF CONTENTS

Pronunciation Guide

a—track	ô—port, fought
ā—mate	ōō—proof
ä—father	u—pun
â—care	ŭ—full
e—pet	ū—you
ē—be	û—purr
i—bit	ə—about, system, supper, circus
ī—bite	oi—toy
o—job	th—thin
ō—wrote	th—there
	zh — vision

Rhetorical Devices

Allusion (a loo´ zhin)

Amplification (âmp li fi kā´ shun)

Anadiplosis (an ə di plō´ sis)

Analogy (a nal´ ə jē)

Anaphora (a naf´ ə r ə)

Antanagoge (an tan ə gō´ jē)

Antithesis (an tith´ ə sis)

Aporia (ə pôr´ ē ə)

Apostrophe (a pos´ trə fē)

Asyndeton (ā sin´də tän)

Chiasmus (kī az´ məs)

Climax (klī´ max)

Conduplicatio (kän dōōp lə kat´ ē ō)

Distinctio (dis tink´shē ō)

Enumeratio (ē nōō mər ä´ tē ō)

Epistrophe (ə pis´ trə fē)

Epithet (ep´ i thet)

Eponym (ep´ ə nim)

Exemplum (ex zem´ plum)

Hyperbaton (hī pər´ bə tän)

Hyperbole (hī pər´ bə lē)

Hypophora (hī pä´ fə rə)

Litotes (lī tō´ tēz)

Metabasis (met ə bā´ sis)

Metaphor (met´ ə for)

Metonymy (mə tän´ i mē)

Parallelism (pa rə lel iz´ m)

Parataxis (pa rə tax´ is)

Parenthesis (pə ren´ thə sis)

Personification (per son i fi kā´ shun)

Polysyndeton (pä´ lē sin də tän)

Procatalepsis (prō kat ə lep´ sis)

Rhetorical Question

Sententia (sen ten´ shē ə)

Simile (sim´ i lē)

Symploce (sim´ plə sē)

Synecdoche (si nek´ də kē)

Understatement

Zeugma (zōōg´ mə)

INTRODUCTION

What Is Rhetoric?

In reading, speaking, or writing, rhetoric is a tool that enhances composition; its aim is to persuade, to inform, to express a personal thought, or simply to entertain the reader. What the formal study of rhetoric allows us to do is isolate exactly what it is we've done so that in the future we can do it again for a similar effect. Rather than haphazardly casting words on the page, letting our vague expectations guide us, we can carefully construct our writing, effectively using the rhetorical devices we have learned.

Although there are literally hundreds of figures of rhetoric, ranging from *anadiplosis* to *zeugma*, some are so rare that you are unlikely to run into them, while others, such as *hyperbole* and *metaphor*, are so common that it is rare to see a newspaper article or hear a speech in which they are not frequently used. For our purpose we will consider 33 of the most useful rhetorical devices.

Keep in mind, however, when using figures of rhetoric, it is important to make sure you are helping your cause, rather than hindering it. A misused form, or a form used in an inappropriate place, can act as an obstacle to your readers, breaking the flow of your argument or actively confusing them about your meaning.

Rhetorical Devices that Help with Strategy

As a writer, you'll want to use rhetorical devices to help strengthen the strategy of your paper. Some of these devices are meant as transitional tools, to help you move seamlessly from one portion of your essay to another, while others are meant to help you present your evidence or information as strongly as possible. Still others help link the entire essay together, making it cohesive and intentional—characteristics valued by the scorers of large-scale writing assessments.

Rhetorical Devices that Help with Style

Whereas strategy and organization are the walls and foundation of an essay, style is the decoration, much like the paint, the wallpaper, and the furniture one might place in a house. Your style will say a lot about your personality and will also reveal your attitude toward the subject and your attitude toward the reader. It can mean the difference between an essay that people read once and forget, or one you clip out of a magazine or newspaper and read over and over. Poor style might mean that no one will ever read the entire essay. It can also mean the difference between a clear, lucid argument, and one that is almost impossible for the reader to understand. Therefore, the stylistic devices that you choose will have a powerful effect, one way or another, on the reception that your writing receives.

EXAMPLES OF RHETORICAL PITFALLS

One of the most useful and versatile rhetorical devices is the *metaphor*. A *metaphor* connects one subject with another that may not be obviously related. When used correctly, it allows the writer to do this in a way that is both stylistically pleasing and concise.

The following quotation has been edited and altered so that it includes a misused *metaphor*. It is from Pope John Paul II, discussing the Nazi Holocaust and the long-lasting impact it has had on Europe:

> Here, as at Auschwitz and many other
> places in Europe, we are overcome by the
> **echo** of the **tears** of so many. Men, women,
> and children cry out to us from the depths
> of the horror that they knew. How can we
> fail to heed their cry? No one can forget or
> ignore what happened. No one can diminish
> its scale.

Note that a *metaphor* is introduced in the first sentence—the idea of the past at Auschwitz and other death camps echoing down through the ages. However, it is then immediately connected with a subject—tears—that cannot echo. This problem is commonly referred to as mixing *metaphors*, and using *metaphors* in this way can cause your reader a great deal of confusion or hilarity, which does not serve the subject. At the very least, it can break the flow of a good *metaphor* by introducing an impossible image that your reader can't correctly visualize.

Another commonly used rhetorical device is *parallelism*. This device connects parts of a sentence, or longer pieces, by using the same structure throughout. *Parallelism* is often used to build force through repetition. It is commonly found in political speeches, as well as religious texts such as the Bible. The benefits of well-used *parallelism* can easily be lost, however, by failing to properly match the form between each element.

Look, for example, at the following quotation from former President George W. Bush, talking about his old friends from Texas and the importance they hold in his life:

> I like my buddies from west Texas. I liked
> them when I was young, I liked them when
> I was middle-age, I liked them before I was
> president, and I like them during president,
> and I like them after president.

Clearly, President Bush switches forms between the first two listed items—having to do with age—and the last three—having to do with his serving as president. He also uses an incorrect verb tense later in the sentence, a result of trying to hold too strictly to the parallel form. Rather than building force, this incomplete *parallelism* seems to stumble over itself in the middle and finishes with a grammatically flawed phrase.

These examples illustrate how incorrectly applied rhetorical devices can confuse your readers or detract from the strength of your statement. When properly applied, however, both *metaphor* and *parallelism* can lend great power to your writing.

While Pope John Paul II's quotation about the Holocaust was altered to include a misused *metaphor*, the actual quotation makes excellent use of the *metaphor*.

> Here, as at Auschwitz and many other places
> in Europe, we are overcome by the echo of
> the heart-rending laments of so many. Men,
> women, and children cry out to us from the
> depths of the horror that they knew. How
> can we fail to heed their cry? No one can
> forget or ignore what happened. No one can
> diminish its scale.

The Pope's *metaphor* evokes the heart-rending wails and cries of those who died during the Shoah, echoing down to us through the ages. By using the *metaphor* of an echo, John Paul II makes us see this pain as something that will continue for a long time to come. At the same time, he reminds us of real laments that real victims made. John Paul II continues his *metaphor* in the following sentences, having the victims "cry out" from the "depths," a placement that is both figurative of the darkness and horror they experienced and evocative of an echoing cry. He then finishes by stating the literal truth behind his *metaphor*: like an echo, it will continue to sound out in the future. Of course, John Paul II could have left out his *metaphor*, telling us simply that no one could forget or ignore the great horrors that occurred during WWII. However, by linking it to such strong imagery, he ensures we will hear what he has to say with the force and power it deserves.

We can easily change what President Bush said, to better convey his meaning and to strengthen the sound of his statement. There are two distinct *parallelisms* at work here, each of which would be better served by standing alone. One way of rewriting it would be:

> I like my buddies from west Texas. I liked
> them when I was young, I liked them when
> I was middle-aged, and I'll like them when
> I'm old.

This option takes the first two listed items of the original quotation—both having to do with his age when he knew his friends—and rounds them out with a final item that keeps the same age-related pattern. It might be preferable to change the middle list item to "I like them now that I'm middle-aged," as well, but we can give President Bush the benefit of the doubt here and leave his original words where possible. Another way of reforming the quotation would be to focus on the last three list items:

> I like my buddies from west Texas. I liked
> them before I was president, I like them now
> that I am president, and I'll like them after
> I've been president.

Look at the different benefits each of these constructions offers. In the first example, by eliminating references to the presidency, we strengthen the effect of the *parallelism*. In the second example, we clarify that President Bush's position has not affected his friendships. Both make good use of the device of *parallelism*, and both accomplish President Bush's aim: to inform his listeners about his loyalty to his friends.

THE FOUR AIMS OF RHETORIC

To Persuade

Persuasion is one of the oldest, and perhaps the most recognized, uses of rhetoric. Because of the way in which many rhetorical devices affect readers, you are offered an opportunity to subtly guide their perspective in ways often barred in a direct approach. By arousing an emotional response, evoking powerful imagery, or calling upon reputable authorities, rhetoric gives you a great deal of power with which to communicate your message.

It is no coincidence that the two groups who use rhetoric the most are also the two groups the most interested in persuading others: politicians and lawyers. Look at almost any political speech written in the past few hundred years, and you'll find many clever uses of rhetoric, for a good lawyer or politician wields rhetoric like a surgeon wields a scalpel: with education, with confidence, and with precision.

Many of the rhetorical devices covered in this book are used to persuade a reader. Some, such as an *exemplum* (citing examples) come naturally when crafting an argument, while others, such as *sententia* (quoting wise sayings) build from this common-sense approach and help to bolster your credibility. In a larger sense, nearly every rhetorical device can be seen as a way of helping to persuade; by improving style, by entertaining the reader, and by organizing thoughts, rhetorical devices can make an argument stronger and more convincing.

To Inform

While rhetoric may not be as visible in its informative uses as it is when being used to persuade, it still serves a vital function. If you look at writing that has helped you learn about something, or if you focus on a specific teacher's methods during class, you will likely come across many of the devices outlined in this book. Similarly, you undoubtedly use tools of rhetoric when you're teaching others or trying to explain a concept to someone else. We have all used the *metaphor* to make a difficult concept a bit more accessible, and there are many other devices that come just as naturally when trying to inform.

To Express

Essays written to express tend to be much less formal than those meant to inform, although the goal is similar. You will often be asked to express your personal thoughts on something—in a college entrance essay, for example. Using rhetorical devices can ensure that your ideas shine.

While you don't need to actually convince your readers of your ideas when writing an essay to express, you do need to persuade them that your ideas are worth reading. Your style of writing will play a large part in doing this, and using rhetorical devices concerned with style will help draw in your reader. The way in which you structure your essay is also very important when writing to express yourself. Expressive essays run the risk of coming across as rambling and incoherent, but by using established rhetorical forms, you can build your ideas on a solid structure. A mastery of rhetoric can help turn expressive essays into gems of writing that others will be excited to read.

To Entertain

In addition to the three purposes already mentioned, you may write something with the primary intent of entertaining your reader.

Sweeping your reader away in your story or essay is often viewed as some sort of innate ability. We often talk about a "gift" when it comes to writing to entertain, even while accepting that other forms of essays can be taught. In truth, writing to entertain is no different. Good writers use rhetorical devices to pull their readers in, to make them laugh, and to make them cry. While it is undoubtedly true that some great writers use rhetoric without a conscious understanding of what they're doing, most writers have studied these forms and know quite well what they're writing.

Writing to entertain is fundamentally about taking your readers where you want them to go. For a well-trained writer, any subject should be able to provoke a predetermined response in a reader. The main difference between a tragedy about war (*For Whom the Bell Tolls*) and a dark comedy about war (*Catch-22*) is its presentation. By using a certain set of rhetorical devices in one way, a story can be dark and moving, but by using them in a different way, the same story can be transformed into a comedy. Told in a third way, the story might switch the reader's emotions back and forth between sadness and laughter.

Entertainment is a valuable weapon in your arsenal to educate, to persuade, or to express yourself. Rarely will you be called upon to write an essay or prose fiction where entertainment will not help your cause.

POPULAR RHETORICAL DEVICES

STRATEGY

Device #1 | ***Hyperbole:***

This is the most popular and commonly used rhetorical device in the entire world of rhetorical devices!

Hyperbole is a powerful rhetorical form when used properly, but a terrible distraction when used improperly. It consists of exaggerating some part of your statement in order to give it emphasis or focus. *Hyperbole* is never meant to be understood literally by the reader, and you should take great care to make sure its intent is apparent. There are few things more damaging to a writer's credibility than having *hyperbole* mistaken for fact, which destroys the point of the *hyperbole*. Consider these two examples of *hyperbole*: "*What is causing the biggest problem is that there are over three billion people on the planet,*" and "*The planet is getting so crowded we may have to take turns sitting down.*" The first may seem hyperbolic, but it merely states a fact; the second, on the other hand, is a fine example of *hyperbole*. It states the same basic idea in a way that is consciously exaggerated for effect.

Hyperbole is the single-most overused rhetorical form. People use it in everyday speech, in writing, and in any form of discourse they happen upon. We are a culture absorbed by exaggeration, and, left unchecked, it can weaken your writing immensely. If you find yourself using *hyperbole* as a way to avoid using actual figures, or to fill space, rethink your strategy.

There are three main uses of *hyperbole*. Each of our examples that follow will demonstrate one of these uses. The first example shows how to use it when you want to make a point strongly; for instance, apply *hyperbole* if you desire to energize your statement and drive it home with gusto.

> *Example #1: "There are more reasons for NASA to fund a trip to Jupiter than there are miles in the journey."*

The next example shows how to use *hyperbole* when you want your reader to snap to attention and focus on what you're writing. It can be used to break the trance your reader has fallen into—as a wake-up call, or a tap on the shoulder. Often *hyperbole*, through *metaphor*, accomplishes this purpose best, although many authors enjoy using tongue-in-cheek *hyperbole*.

> *Example #2: "At these words, the people became so silent you could hear a beating heart from across the room."*

The third example shows how to use it as a way of demonstrating the difference between two things. Note how hyperbole can be used to exaggerate differences.

> *Example #3:* *"Compared to the world during the last Ice Age, a Minnesota winter feels like spring in Hawaii."*

Exercise 1:

Write a statement using *hyperbole* about the following topics; consider the best and worst thing you could say about the topic, then exaggerate your statement. *The first one has been done for you as an example.*

Answers will vary, but each statement must be a blatant exaggeration—a *hyperbole*.

1. **My neighborhood**
   Statement: **My neighborhood is so boring that when a cat walks across the street, it draws a crowd.**

2. school in general
   Statement:

3. a friend's athletic ability
   Statement:

4. the weather
   Statement:

5. your favorite or least favorite team
   Statement:

6. a television show
   Statement:

7. a musical group
   Statement:

Device #2   **Understatement:**

You might find this device somewhat helpful as well.

Understatement is a rhetorical form in which the force of a descriptive statement is *less* than what one would normally expect. When describing a category five hurricane, for example, one might describe it simply as "a bit of weather." *Understatement* can be used either to highlight the extreme nature of the event, or for ironic effect, as in, *"Leonardo da Vinci had a good idea or two."*

In some cases, *understatement* is the best way to demonstrate how powerful an event or idea actually is. In essence, you signal to the reader that the concept itself is so self-explanatory that there is nothing you can add to its force with superfluous words. By understating the case, readers are prompted to think how much more could be said—and by making them come to the conclusion themselves, you make that conclusion all the more powerful.

In other cases, repeated use of *understatement* can lull a reader into a sense of calm. When you then reveal the true extent of what you have been under-representing, it will have an added emphasis. This style of understating something for the sake of later driving the point home forcefully is particularly useful when building an argument to convince.

Understatement may also be used for humorous effect. When contrasted sharply with reality, a statement can have such an absurd meaning that a listener or reader cannot help but laugh. It should not, however, be confused with simplifying a discussion or idea. While simplification aims to make something more understandable, or easier to talk about, *understatement* is trying to bring out the full force of an idea. Overly simplifying something in an essay can weaken your case, while *understatement* used properly will strengthen it.

> *Example #1:* *"Whatever his faults, Sir Isaac Newton did have a fairly good mind for science."*

> *Example #2:* *"The Middle East is currently having some political squabbles."*

> *Example #3:* *"To the uninitiated, neurophysiology can be a bit of a challenge."*

Exercise 1:

Write 5 satiric comments that include understatement by completing the following sentences. *The first one has been done for you as an example.*

Answers will vary, but they must be *understatements*.

1. Our school <u>spirit is, shall we say, less than overwhelmingly enthusiastic.</u>

2. The meal was

3. Our team

4. That television show was

5. The band is

6. As a performer

Exercise 2:

The following passage comes from Jonathan Swift's essay "A Modest Proposal." This essay uses a number of devices to satirize the apparent English indifference to the poverty-stricken condition of their Irish subjects. Consider the essay's title and the outrageous solution he proposes. In the following paragraphs, identify how Swift uses understatement to advance his point. Is his understatement effective here? Why or why not?

Answers will vary.

It is a melancholy object to those who walk through this great town or travel in the country, when they see the streets, the roads, and cabin doors, crowded with beggars of the female sex, followed by three, four, or six children, all in rags and importuning every passenger for an alms....

The number of souls in this kingdom being usually reckoned one million and a half, of these I calculate there may be about two hundred thousand couple whose wives are breeders; from which number I subtract thirty thousand couple, who are able to maintain their own children, (although I apprehend there cannot be so many, under the present distresses of the kingdom) but this being granted, there will remain an hundred and seventy thousand breeders. I again subtract fifty thousand, for those women who miscarry, or whose children die by accident or disease within the year. There only remain an hundred and twenty thousand children of poor parents annually born. The question therefore is, How this number shall be reared, and provided for? which, as I have already said, under the present situation of affairs, is utterly impossible by all the methods hitherto proposed. For we can neither employ them in handicraft or agriculture; we neither build houses, (I mean in the country) nor cultivate land: they can very seldom pick up a livelihood by stealing till they arrive at six years old; except where they are of towardly parts, although I confess they learn the rudiments much earlier; during which time they can however be properly looked upon only as probationers: As I have been informed by a principal gentleman in the county of Cavan, who protested to me, that he never knew above one or two instances under the age of six, even in a part of the kingdom so renowned for the quickest proficiency in that art....

I shall now therefore humbly propose my own thoughts, which I hope <u>will not be liable to the least objection</u>.

I have been assured by a very knowing American of my acquaintance in London, <u>that a young healthy child well nursed is at a year old a most delicious, nourishing, and wholesome food, whether stewed, roasted, baked, or boiled; and I make no doubt that it will equally serve in a fricassee or a ragout</u>....

Swift uses understated facts and opinions to demonstrate to the reader the absurdity of his suggestion. The concept itself— eating poor children for food for the rich—is so hyperbolic that *understatement* proves to be quite effective in developing the satire.

Device #3

Litotes:

What you'll learn in this section isn't bad.

Litotes, similar to understatement, emphasizes its point by using a word opposite to the condition. For example, rather than say, *"The trip across the mountain was a hard journey,"* we may say, *"The trip was no easy journey."* Due to the unexpectedness of the latter sentence, it can have more force and power than the former. Mere understatement would have the sentence read, *"The journey was easy."* The difference lies in the way the sentence is constructed and in the direction of the emphasis.

Litotes is often combined with understatement to further emphasize something. This can be seen in certain uses of a phrase like, *"It wasn't a bad deal,"* for example, as a way of describing the Louisiana Purchase. Often speakers will use *litotes* as understatement in describing their own achievements, so as not to seem arrogant. A father may describe his child's graduating *magna cum laude* from Harvard as "no small accomplishment," to emphasize the importance of the feat.

Litotes may also be used to weaken a claim. While an obviously ironic use of *litotes* acts as an understatement to emphasize the initial claim, a non-ironic use can soften the edges of that same claim. This is especially true when dealing with negative words like "bad" or "weak." Instead of saying, *"It was a good day,"* for example, we could say, *"It wasn't a bad day."* While the first statement has a definite meaning—the day was good— the second statement is a bit less clear. It could mean the day was good, but it could also mean the day wasn't good or bad, but somewhere in between. *Litotes* allows the writer to say what *isn't* true, without committing as strongly to what *is* true.

> *Example #1: "A cup of coffee would not be unwelcome."*

> *Example #2: "It's not the smartest idea I've ever heard."*

> *Example #3: "That store is not in the most convenient location."*

Exercise 1:

Write 5 original statements that use *litotes* to emphasize a point or startle a reader into paying attention. *The first one has been done for you as an example.*

Answers will vary, but they must be *litotes*.

1. The former CEO's lifestyle was not shabby, which may explain why the company went bankrupt.

2.

3.

4.

5.

6.

Exercise 2:

In your own words, rewrite each of the following examples of *litotes* as straight declarative statements. Try to keep the style of the original.

Answers will vary.

1. "...I will multiply them, and they shall not be few; I will make them honored, and they shall not be small." (Jeremiah 30:19 RSV)

   "...They shall be very many, and they shall be very great."

2. "That [sword] was not useless / to the warrior now." (*Beowulf*)

   "The sword was useful."

3. "It isn't very serious. I have this tiny little tumor on the brain." (*The Catcher in the Rye*)

   "The brain tumor is serious."

4. "for life's not a paragraph/And death I think is no parenthesis"

   (*e e cummings*)

   "Death is longer than life, and I think life is too short to allow death to intrude."

Device #4

Antithesis:

A fairly simple way to show a complex thought.

Antithesis makes use of a contrast in language to bring out a contrast in ideas. It is one of the most attractive and powerful tools in speech and writing. Some of the most famous lines in modern history are built on the *antithesis,* from Neil Armstrong's *"That's one small step for [a] man, one giant leap for mankind,"* to Martin Luther King, Jr.'s *"...not be judged by the color of their skin but by the content of their character."* Antithesis has a natural beauty to the human ear because we are creatures who love to organize and categorize our thoughts and ideas. *Antithesis* organizes ideas in a way that is both evocative and powerful, and it is an excellent tool to have in your writer's toolbox.

Antithesis can be built by contrasting any of the different parts of a statement.

- You may wish to keep the structure of the sentences identical, but use two opposing words.
- You may wish to change entire clauses to contrast with one another.
- You may even wish to have whole sentences oppose one another throughout the course of a paragraph. While simply opposing a key word can be the easiest to build, longer uses of *antithesis* can be very powerful.

The sound of a sentence built on *antithesis* can also be used to great effect. Trying to alliterate, or match the first sound of the contrasting words, can help highlight the opposition. For example:

> *"Life can be kind and cruel, full of hope and heartache,"*

can drive the point home more eloquently than:

> *"Life can be kind and mean, full of joy and heartache."*

Antithesis can also help to point out fine distinctions in an issue by presenting them together. By contrasting legality and morality, wisdom and learning, or success and happiness, you make your reader think about the subtle shades of difference between the concepts. When dealing with ideas that you think your reader might tend to think of as the same, joining them in *antithesis* can help set the stage for your argument.

> *Example #1:* "*We live within our limits, for we are men, not gods.*"

> *Example #2:* "*I speak not from ignorance, but from experience.*"

> *Example #3:* "*War is not fought to achieve joy, but rather to avoid pain.*"

Exercise 1:

Write 5 original statements that use *antithesis* to emphasize a point or startle a reader into paying attention. *The first one has been done for you as an example.*

Answers will vary, but they must be *antitheses*.

1. The villain lives by his wits, not by his labor.

2.

3.

4.

5.

6.

Exercise 2:

For each famous quote, underline the specific words and phrases that are being contrasted by *antithesis*.

1. "We are caught in <u>war</u>, wanting <u>peace</u>. We are torn by <u>division,</u> wanting <u>unity</u>." —Richard Nixon

2. "If a free society cannot help the <u>many</u> who are <u>poor</u>, it cannot save the <u>few</u> who are <u>rich</u>."—John F. Kennedy

3. Marc Antony: "I came to <u>bury</u> Caesar, not to <u>praise</u> him."—Shakespeare (*Julius Caesar*)

4. "I pass with relief from the <u>tossing sea</u> of <u>Cause and Theory</u> to the <u>firm ground</u> of <u>Result and Fact.</u>" —Winston Churchill

5. "<u>Extremism</u> in defense of liberty is no <u>vice</u>, <u>moderation</u> in the pursuit of justice is no <u>virtue</u>." —Barry Goldwater

6. Brutus: "Not that I loved Caesar <u>less</u>, but that I loved Rome <u>more</u>." —Shakespeare (*Julius Caesar*)

7. "It was the <u>best of times</u>, it was the <u>worst of times</u>, it was the <u>age of wisdom</u>, it was the <u>age of foolishness</u>..." —Charles Dickens (*A Tale of Two Cities*)

8. "Too <u>black</u> for <u>heaven</u>, and yet too <u>white</u> for <u>hell</u>." —John Dryden (*The Hind and the Panther*)

9. "To <u>err</u> is <u>human</u>, to <u>forgive</u>, <u>divine</u>." —Alexander Pope (*An Essay on Criticism*)

10. "<u>Fair</u> is <u>foul</u>, and <u>foul</u> is <u>fair</u>." —Shakespeare (*Macbeth*)

Device #5   ***Hypophora:***

So what is this? Read on, and you will see.

Hypophora is the technique of asking a question, then proceeding to answer it. While the name is certainly a mouthful, *hypophora* is one of the most useful strategic devices when writing essays to inform or persuade. For example, many politicians make it a staple of their press conferences, often to such a degree that they have been mocked by the press. A mayor might say, *"Why am I for putting more police officers on the streets? Their presence prevents crime."* Used appropriately, however, *hypophora* can accomplish a wide range of objectives with minimal effort.

Perhaps the most common use of *hypophora* is in a standard-format essay, to introduce a paragraph. A writer will begin the paragraph with a question, and then use the remaining space to answer that question. For example, *"Why should you vote for me? I'll give you five good reasons...."* This can be a good way to guide your readers from point to point to make sure they're able to follow.

Hypophora can also be used as a way to anticipate questions or concerns you think your reader might raise. By addressing these concerns directly, you help strengthen your case. By phrasing them first in the form of questions, you make it clear that you understand your reader's thought process, as in this example: *"So what is the answer to our rising crime problem?"* Used in this way, *hypophora* feels very natural and easy, and it serves as a way to help your reader feel directly connected and involved in the discussion.

In some cases, you might suspect that your readers might know too little about your topic to know which pertinent questions to ask. *Hypophora* can help introduce them to important information without making it seem as if you're forcing it upon them. Phrasing it as a question leads your readers to feel as if they thought of it—making your answer then seem like something they always wanted to know. The use of *hypophora* as a tool for suggestion can be incredibly powerful when used well, subtly shifting the direction of your reader's thought.

Rather than asking a single question and answering that question, you may wish to use *hypophora* to bring up a number of points. The most effective way to do this is to ask a series of questions that are related, and then spend some time addressing the underlying concern. While it would be possible to address each question individually, this can bore your reader and feel contrived. By reducing a group of questions to one broader point, you are able to advance the point more effectively.

*Example #1: "How do we know this to be true? We have
observed it in the lab."*

*Example #2: "What then of the future? Let come what
may, and we shall meet it without fear."*

*Example #3: "Do we then submit to our oppressor? No.
No. A thousand times, no."*

Exercise 1:

The following passages are from "Letter from Birmingham Jail," written
by Dr. Martin Luther King, Jr. There are very few question marks in the
paragraphs, yet Dr. King has effectively used *hypophora* through implied
questions and answers. Read this excerpt and underline all instances of
hypophora.

While confined here in the Birmingham city jail, I came across your
recent statement calling my present activities "unwise and untimely."
Seldom do I pause to answer criticism of my work and ideas. If I
sought to answer all the criticisms that cross my desk, my secretaries
would have little time for anything other than such correspondence
in the course of the day, and I would have no time for constructive
work. But since I feel that you are men of genuine good will and
that your criticisms are sincerely set forth, **I want to try to answer
your statements in what I hope will be patient and reasonable
terms.**

**I think I should indicate why I am here in Birmingham, since
you have been influenced by the view which argues against
"outsiders coming in." I have the honor of serving as president
of the Southern Christian Leadership Conference**, an organization
operating in every southern state, with headquarters in Atlanta,
Georgia. We have some eighty-five affiliated organizations across
the South, and one of them is the Alabama Christian Movement for
Human Rights. Frequently we share staff, educational and financial
resources with our affiliates. **Several months ago the affiliate here
in Birmingham asked us to be on call to engage in a nonviolent
direct-action program if such were deemed necessary. We readily
consented, and when the hour came we lived up to our promise. So
I, along with several members of my staff, am here because I was**

invited here. I am here because I have organizational ties here.

But more basically, I am in Birmingham because injustice is here. Just as the prophets of the eighth century B.C. left their villages and carried their "thus saith the Lord" far beyond the boundaries of their home towns, and just as the Apostle Paul left his village of Tarsus and carried the gospel of Jesus Christ to the far corners of the Greco-Roman world, **so am I compelled to carry the gospel of freedom beyond my own home town**. Like Paul, I must constantly respond to the Macedonian call for aid.... **You deplore the demonstrations taking place in Birmingham. But your statement, I am sorry to say, fails to express a similar concern for the conditions that brought about the demonstrations**. I am sure that none of you would want to rest content with the superficial kind of social analysis that deals merely with effects and does not grapple with underlying causes. It is unfortunate that demonstrations are taking place in Birmingham, but it is even more unfortunate that the city's white power structure left the Negro community with no alternative....

You may well ask: "Why direct action? Why sit-ins, marches and so forth? Isn't negotiation a better path?" You are quite right in calling, for negotiation. Indeed, this is the very purpose of direct action. Nonviolent direct action seeks to create such a crisis and foster such a tension that a community which has constantly refused to negotiate is forced to confront the issue. It seeks so to dramatize the issue that it can no longer be ignored.

Exercise 2:

For each of the following questions, write an answer that could be used to complete the *hypophora*. *The first one has been done for you as an example.*

Answers will vary. However, they must relate to the question.

1. Why should you vote in the next election?
   Your future may depend on who is elected.

2. What are "American values"?

3. What must we do to get good government?

4. Why should we cut taxes?

5. Why is it better to love than be loved?

6. So you ask, "How are humans really that different from other animals?"

Device #6

Rhetorical Question:

Don't you want to know how to use them well?

The *rhetorical question* is something of a cousin to *hypophora*. While a *hypophora* asks a question and then answers it immediately, a *rhetorical question* is one in which the answer is merely implied. It is used effectively in the following example from John Milton: *"For what can war but endless war breed?"* Hypophora offers the writer an opportunity to tell readers something they *don't* know; a *rhetorical question* gives the writer an opportunity to highlight something readers *do* know.

While every strategic device runs the risk of being used in a lazy or inappropriate way, the *rhetorical question* is especially tempting. Before using a *rhetorical question*, make sure to ask what purpose it is going to serve. Too often a *rhetorical question* is used as an easy replacement for a strong introduction to a thought. When used correctly, however, a *rhetorical question* should make the reader pause for thought or it should drive your point home with gusto. The point should not just slide unnoticed into the next sentence. In fact, while you may be tempted to begin paragraphs with rhetorical questions, keep in mind that this form can often be used most effectively to conclude a point.

Usually, a *rhetorical question* is phrased in such a way that it requires either a simple "yes" or "no" answer. While it is possible to have rhetorical questions with more in-depth answers, you need to make sure that the answer is as apparent to your readers as it is to you. Even in the case of a "yes" or "no," make sure your readers know how they should answer. Asking an ambiguous question that people could easily respond to in either way can have disastrous consequences for the rest of your essay. Once you lose your reader's faith, it will be very difficult to regain it. With questions that could be answered either positively or negatively, ensure that you have given your readers enough information in the previous paragraphs or sentences that they know how you expect them to respond. Since, unlike the *hypophora*, the *rhetorical question* does *not* supply its own answer, be careful *never* to use this strategy unless you are *absolutely certain* that the answer your readers will supply is the one you *want* them to supply.

Like the *hypophora*, however, a well-used *rhetorical question* will engage and excite your readers. By leading them to their own discovery of the point you want to make, you strengthen that point's impact tenfold. For this reason, the *rhetorical question* is best kept in reserve—to emphasize your most crucial points. Overusing *rhetorical questions* will weaken their effectiveness, leaving them less effective when you truly have need of one.

*Example #1: "In this age of modernity, can we truly
condone such horrific acts?"*

*Example #2: "How can we expect a man to give more
than we ourselves are willing to give?"*

*Example #3: "Do you want a world in which those
dearest to you can know peace and safety
or a world in which every moment carries
with it the constant fear of death?"*

Exercise 1:

Write 5 original *rhetorical questions* to help your readers arrive at—and agree with—the point to which you have been leading them. *The first one has been done for you as an example.*

Answers will vary, but they must be *rhetorical questions.*

1. Why should we *not* protest the selling of our natural resources to the highest bidder?

2.

3.

4.

5.

6.

Device #7   **Procatalepsis:**

Some will insist that the formal study of rhetoric is unnecessary.

Procatalepsis is another relative of the *hypophora*. While the *hypophora* can ask any sort of question, the *procatalepsis* deals specifically with objections, and it usually does so without even asking the question, as in this example: *"Many other experts want to classify Sanskrit as an extinct language, but I do not."* By directly addressing objections, *procatalepsis* lets the writer further his or her argument and satisfy readers at the same time. Strategically, *procatalepsis* shows your readers that you have anticipated their concerns, and have already thought them through. It is, therefore, especially effective in argumentative essays.

Procatalepsis can be used in many different ways. First, determine what the most likely, common, or troubling objections to your argument are, then offer strong answers to those objections. Take care that your answers fully address the initial objection.

Second, you may come up with your own arguments, specifically to bolster your central point. Make sure the objections are actually plausible and not obviously set up just for you to knock down. By coming up with potential problems for which you already have a clear answer, you make it appear that the point you are trying to defend has been well thought-out and can withstand criticism.

Third, some writers take this a step further and write as though their contrived objection is held by a certain type of person. They make the objection more pertinent by attributing it to people in a certain economic, social, or moral bracket. This can be an incredibly powerful tool, but you need to be cautious in using it. Setting up a theoretical objector who is too absurd, or too unbelievable—commonly referred to as a straw man—will weaken your argument.

Procatalepsis can even be used if you don't have a full answer to the objection. By being honest about the fact that there are problems with your argument, you show your audience that you are grounded in reality. You should never, however, bring up an objection to which you have no response. Indeed, if you are aware of too many objections to which you cannot respond, you probably already know that the point you are arguing is not that compelling. State the objection, admit its merits, and then go on to discuss why the positive outcome of your argument outweighs the legitimate concerns.

Example #1: *"There are those who would say the American people could never make such sacrifices. To them I say: have we forgotten World War II so soon? Let us remember the rationing of tin and milk, of copper and eggs. Let us remember the hours spent in prayer, at work, and in battle on the front. Let us remember a people coming together for one noble purpose, and making whatever sacrifices were needed to achieve that common goal."*

Example #2: *"This is an objection one often hears raised by certain people—usually liberal to a fault, frightened of their own shadow, and worried about doing anything that may be interpreted as aggressive. We can respect their concerns, but at the same time, must recognize that they are not our own."*

Example #3: *"It may be pointed out that the proposed tax plan adds a burden to a small number of families in the upper brackets. While this may be true, the benefits offered to those who are most in need must surely outweigh a small bit of hardship to those who are not."*

Exercise 1:

Find an editorial in your local newspaper about a topic that interests you. Write a brief essay in response to that editorial, and use at least 3 examples of *procatalepsis* in your writing.

Answers will vary, but they must be *procatalepsis.*

Exercise 2:

Write 5 original statements using *procatalepsis* to support and emphasize your point. *The first one has been done for you as an example.*

Answers will vary, but they must be *procatalepsis*.

1. Some people, even in this era of modern thought, believe that UFOs are visiting our planet every day, but without tangible evidence, mere belief is not proof.

2.

3.

4.

5.

6.

Exercise 3:

For each issue, write two objections that your opponent might raise. Then, give a brief statement showing how you would refute them.

Answers will vary. Students should provide logical oppositions and rebuttals.

Example:
Issue: Gasoline taxes should be raised to cut down on driving and air pollution.

Opposition (A):   This would unfairly affect the poor since they can afford any increase much less than rich people can, yet they must still drive the same distances they do now.

Rebuttal (A):   In the long run, the benefits from extra taxes will help the poor more, not less, than the rich; the poor will save on health care, they will pay less insurance, and helping the environment definitely aids the poor more than it does the rich.

Opposition (B):   Americans are taxed too much already.

Rebuttal (B):   In comparison to citizens in many other countries, like Sweden, Austria, or Belgium, the U.S. taxpayer pays a smaller percentage of his or her salary to the government.

1.   Issue: Nuclear bombs should be banned in all countries.

   Opposition (A):

   Rebuttal (A):

   Opposition (B):

   Rebuttal (B):

2. Issue: All forms of religious expression should be banned/recognized in public schools. (choose either "banned" or "recognized")

Opposition (A):

Rebuttal (A):

Opposition (B):

Rebuttal (B):

3. Issue: Schools should not be cutting back on money for music and art, they should be spending more.

Opposition (A):

Rebuttal (A):

Opposition (B):

Rebuttal (B):

4. Issue: Animal testing should be abolished.

Opposition (A):

Rebuttal (A):

Opposition (B):

Rebuttal (B):

5. Issue: Violent movies adversely influence adolescents.

Opposition (A):

Rebuttal (A):

Opposition (B):

Rebuttal (B):

Device #8   *Distinctio:*

This will be a most informative section—informative in the sense that you will learn some new ideas, as well as clarify some things you might have thought you already knew.

Distinctio is a rhetorical form in which the writer elaborates on the definition of a word, to make sure there is no misunderstanding. Here is an example: *"Before we can discuss immigration, we need to agree on the fact that there are huge differences between legal and illegal immigration."* Words can be slippery creatures, and in English especially, they can have many meanings. *Distinctio* allows you to tell your reader exactly what you mean to say. This sort of clarification can be the difference between your sentence being understood or being taken to mean something entirely different from what you intended.

Words that indicate how *good* something is, how *likely* something is, or how *difficult* something is—these are all words that often need clarification. There are also a number of concepts that have words attached to them whose meanings are hotly debated—democracy and freedom are two good examples. If you fail to convey your intended meaning of the word, your readers will be left on their own to decide.

Distinctio is usually used with a linking phrase such as, "which is to say" or "by which I mean." It may also be used by putting a definition in parentheses immediately after the term you're defining, as in this example: *"The most popular Internet search engine (this would be Google, not Yahoo!, the obsolete AltaVista, Wikipedia, or Ask.com) attracts nearly a half billion searches every hour."* Take care to use *distinctio only* when it's actually needed to maintain the integrity of your sentence—an essay riddled with definitions will tend to feel distracted and disjointed to the reader.

Example #1: *"Communism, by which I mean the socialist communalism which comes after the centralized state, has yet to be tried anywhere in the real world."*

Example #2: *"At this point, we have a short time left—a short time being less than fifty years."*

Example #3: *"Is the software easy to use (can my ninety-year-old grandmother learn it) or difficult (do I need a degree in computer science)?"*

Exercise 1:

Write an original statement for each of the following abstract or ambiguous words using *distinctio* to clarify the meaning. *The first one has been done for you as an example.*

Answers will vary.

1. worthwhile: That book was tremendously worthwhile; it taught me all I needed to know about Russia.

2. colorful:

3. deep:

4. work:

5. standard:

6. bright:

7. crazy:

8. smart:

9. common:

10. right:

Exercise 2:

Utilizing various reading materials, such as newspapers, magazines, novels and blogs, identify and list 5 examples of effective *distinctio*. Then identify and list 5 examples of ineffective or unnecessary *distinctio*. Provide an explanation for each answer. *The first one has been done for you as an example.*

Answers will vary, but they must be examples of *distinctio*, and students must offer plausible and thoughtful explanations.

Effective

1. Effective *Distinctio*: *Before we can agree on who is the best shortstop we have to agree on what "best" encompasses; are we talking fielding or hitting—if hitting, are we talking batting average or RBI's?*

   Explanation: *The use of distinctio is effective because the term "best" is too vague a term and different persons with different understandings of the term might not ever find a common ground.*

2. Effective *Distinctio*:

   Explanation:

3. Effective *Distinctio*:

   Explanation:

4. Effective *Distinctio*:

   Explanation:

5. Effective *Distinctio*:

   Explanation:

6. Effective *Distinctio*:

Explanation:

Ineffective

1. Ineffective *Distinctio*: *The red convertible—red the color of an apple, not the red of a traffic light—was sold.*

   Explanation: *This use of* distinctio *is ineffective because distinguishing between the two shades of red adds* nothing *to the sentence.*

2. Ineffective *Distinctio*:

   Explanation:

3. Ineffective *Distinctio*:

   Explanation:

4. Ineffective *Distinctio*:

   Explanation:

5. Ineffective *Distinctio*:

   Explanation:

6. Effective *Distinctio*:

   Explanation:

Device #9

Simile:

A good simile is like a clean window looking into the mind of the writer.

A *simile* is a device in which the writer compares two things that are already somewhat related. For example, if you wanted to describe how the sun lit up a mountain, rather than write, *"The sun lit up the mountain,"* it might sound better to use a *simile*: *"The sun peered, like a curious child, over the top of the mountain."* Since *similes* conjure up strongly suggestive imagery, they lend new details to the main object. The *simile*, one of the more easily recognized rhetorical devices, consists of one noun being compared to another noun and linked by the word "like." The basic form has the key subject first, and the noun that fleshes it out listed second.

> *Example #1: "The shower room, steamy like a Louisiana summer, rang with the athletes' jubilant laughter."*

A *simile* might also flip this order around, with the primary noun coming last. In this case the word "so" is usually used instead of "like."

> *Example #2: "The night is gentle and quiet; so, too, is my love for her."*

A *simile* can also compare two entire phrases, or compare two verbs, in which case the word "as" is used to link them, as in the third example.

> *Example #3: "You should sing tonight as a bird in spring, calling for its mate."*

As well as being linked to each other because one thing is like the other, a *simile* can also connect two things that are barely similar to one another. By pointing out that something is not like, or is unlike, something else, you can tell your reader a great deal about it. You can also use a negative *simile* to connect two things that are actually nothing alike—and keep your credibility by pointing out they *are* nothing alike; this technique will still link the items in your reader's mind.

> *Example #4: "The workday of an Emergency Medical*
> *Technician is not at all like the day of a*
> *nine-to-five office-dweller."*

This *simile* indicates that the differences in the two jobs are greater than the one similarity of them both being daily jobs.

> *Example #5: "Certainly, we know that high school is*
> *not like prison, and a principal is not a*
> *warden."*

This *simile*, however, forces the reader to focus on the similarities between a jail and a school, rather than on the differences between them.

    While the *simile* has many stylistic uses, its strategic value should not be underestimated. The ability to create images and new associations in your reader's mind is an important one, and the *simile* offers an easy way to do just this. *Similes* are common enough that they don't break the flow of your essay, but have enough flexibility that you can make them do virtually anything you need them to do.

Exercise 1:

The *simile* appears frequently in poetry, but is common in all types of writing, both formal and informal. Using any type of writing you encounter, identify and list examples of *simile* usage. Then, explain your interpretation of the writer's intent. *The first one has been done for you as an example.*

Answers will vary, but they must be *similes*, and students must cite source and offer plausible interpretations.

1.   Simile: *"It's a sad, sad state of affairs when Liberals campaign like*
         Republicans to get elected, and Republicans govern like Liberals
         to be loved."
    Source: *Texas Governor Rick Perry*
    Interpretation: *Members of both political parties have compromised on*
               party principles for the sake of their political careers.

2. *Simile*:
   Source:
   Interpretation:

3. *Simile*:
   Source:
   Interpretation:

4. *Simile*:
   Source:
   Interpretation:

5. *Simile*:
   Source:
   Interpretation:

Exercise 2:

Create 5 sentences with *similes* linking the two parts with the word "so," as we did in example #2. *The first one has been done for you as an example.*

1. *"Sugar is sweet, and so are you."*

2.

3.

4.

5.

6.

Exercise 3:

Using the word "as," create 5 sentences as we did in Example #3. *The first one has been done for you as an example.*

1. *"Your words slice my heart as diamonds cut glass."*

2.

3.

4.

5.

6.

Exercise 4:

Follow the directions for each of the following scenarios. Use at least 1 *simile* for each answer, and underline them. *The first one has been done for you as an example.*

Answers will vary. *Similes* must contain "like," "so," or "as" to be correct.

1. Imagine you are on the beach during a tropical storm. Describe the movement of the waves as they come ashore.

    The waves pound the shore <u>like furious horses galloping into battle.</u>

2. Think of your favorite meal. Describe the appearance, taste, texture, and/ or smell of the dish in at least three sentences.

3. Think of a time that you won something—a game, a prize, a bet, etc.— and try to remember how you felt. Now describe your feelings in one sentence.

4. Imagine you are visiting a farm. Think of the animals, crops, and other items that might surround you. Describe your vision of the farm in four sentences.

5. Who is your best friend? Think of the qualities that make him or her special, and describe the person in at least two sentences.

Like a stained glass window, the simile sheds light and color on a piece of writing.

We've already gone over the strategic value of the *simile* in evoking nuance, but the *simile's* real value is in its stylistic grace. *Similes* have the potential to shock and impress us by drawing comparisons we wouldn't have thought of, but which are so eloquent they cannot be ignored.

There is no reason you should limit your use of a *simile* to either a strategic or stylistic purpose. The best *similes* will both advance your cause and be beautiful in their own right. For example, *"Parents are like angels, watching over us in our times of need."* While there is nothing wrong with creating a *simile* just for the sake of form, it is always worth considering how you can tweak it to make it serve a greater function at the same time. For example, *"Loneliness is like the barren tree in winter, awaiting spring."*

When creating a *simile*, a great deal of the style comes from the comparison's unique nature. Present a *simile* that is too common, and it will land flat and make you seem uninspired. The best *similes* surprise, while also seeming natural. In the beginning though, it may help you to fall back on clichéd *similes* you are familiar with, changing them slightly to add a bit of the unexpected, such as, *"Innocent as a newborn baby."* Consider how this phrase might be changed: *"Innocent as a newborn kitten"*; *"Awkward as a newborn baby"*; *"Funny as a toddler's first steps."*

Exercise 5:

Write 6 original *similes*. Remember that the *simile* is not only a way to clarify an idea and imply a value or quality that is difficult to express, but it is also a way to surprise and delight your reader. For 3 of them, you may take a cliché and state it in a different way similar to, *"Innocent as a newborn baby." The first one has been done for you as an example.*

Answers will vary, but they must be valid and original *similes*.

1. *As angry as a bear in a trap, the patient glowered at the committee of doctors.*

2.

3.

4.

5.

6.

7.

Exercise 6:

Write 2 *similes* for each of the following topics. *The first one has been done for you as an example.*

Answers will vary. *Similes* must contain "like," "so," or "as" to be correct.

1. a chain-link fence

   A. *The chain-link fence enclosed the playground like a giant net for children.*

   B.

2. the cries of an infant

   A.

   B.

3. a tennis ball

   A.

   B.

4. a credit card

   A.

   B.

5. ice cream

   A.

   B.

The good, old, reliable simile is like the friend you haven't called in a year, but who'll be the first to show up at your birthday party.

Similes can be a bit tricky to see because they can compare myriad different parts of speech, phrases, or clauses, and, in some cases, longer sentences. The most common form of a *simile* is comparing one noun to another, as in, *"The sun is like a giant burning ball,"* or comparing one noun to a longer noun phrase, as in, *"The sun is like a trillion nuclear bombs going off at once, every second of every day."* In this common usage, the word "like" should be your cue that what you're seeing is a *simile*. Verbs might also be compared to one another, using the word "as" to link them, as in, *"I slept calmly, as a sparrow finding shelter from the storm."*

Not all *similes* are linked by "as" or "like"—in some circumstances other words might link them, and in others the "like" or "as" will be implied. Keep your eyes open for these key words, but also be on a more general lookout for sentences in which an object is compared in a somewhat abstract way to something else. For example, *"When you hear the word 'committee,' you think of a dinosaur: a huge lumbering beast destined to eventually go extinct."* *Similes* also take a negative approach, saying how something is unlike something else. They might also compare the two things, saying how one thing is more than or less than something else.

Example #1: *"The Philadelphia Phillies have less chance of winning a World Series than a plow horse has of winning the Kentucky Derby."*

Example #2: *"The man's joy at finding his wallet was no less than a lottery winner's claiming her prize."*

When you do find a *simile*, first try to determine whether it's being used purely for a stylistic purpose. If the comparison seems to have no bearing on the meaning of either item, this is probably the case. If there seems to be more going on, however, look a little bit deeper to get as much value as possible from the *simile*. Think about what comparisons the writer is most likely trying to get you to make by linking the two items, and think about how this changes your understanding or evaluation of the ideas being compared.

> *Example #3:* *"The sub-committee, like a child afraid of jumping into a cold swimming pool, did nothing throughout the 1980s."*

> *Example #4:* *"We pushed forward through impossible odds, as camels push ever on through the deep desert."*

Exercise 7:

For each group of sentences, identify the letter of the one that is not a *simile*. In addition, some are different rhetorical devices. If so, identify these. *The first one has been done for you as an example.*

1.
   - A. The horse galloped a million miles an hour.
   - B. The horse galloped as swift as a jet plane flies.
   - C. The horse galloped like a Kentucky Derby winner.
   - A. *THIS IS A USE OF HYPERBOLE.*

2.
   - A. The waves rolled to shore like a slinky—back and forth, back and forth.
   - B. Ocean water tastes like salt.
   - C. We rode the waves as the day went on.
   - C. **"AS" HERE IS A CONJUNCTION.**

3.
   - A. This computer is as useless as a headless hammer.
   - B. Our computer is not less than two years old.
   - C. That computer functions no better than a typewriter.
   - B. **NO COMPARISON IS MADE; IT JUST STATES A FACT.**

4.
   - A. Her hair, as golden as the sun, blew into her face.
   - B. Her hair was as tangled as a rat's nest.
   - C. Her hair, a dirty mop, covered her eyes.
   - C. **IT IS A *METAPHOR*.**

5.

    A.   Gazpacho, a tomato-based soup, is served ice cold.

    B.   Gazpacho is not like Campbell's tomato soup.

    C.   Some varieties of gazpacho resemble salsa.

    A.   THERE IS NO COMPARISON HERE.

6.

    A.   The dancer moved like a flower in a springtime breeze.

    B.   The graceful dancer, a butterfly in flight, captivated the audience.

    C.   The dancer was as flexible as a rubber band.

    B.   IT IS A *METAPHOR*.

Recognizing a clever simile is like reuniting with an old friend.

A carefully chosen *simile* can do more than clarify a concept for the reader: it can also create shades of meaning. For example, look at this sentence: *"I'm not sure why her tears were like a river."* If the sentence used *angry* or *jealous tears* or the *river* were *furious* or *slow*, the entire meaning of the sentence would be altered; it is important, therefore, to be mindful of word choices when *simile* is involved.

A well-written *simile* will both clarify a point and strike the reader as stylistically elegant and beautiful. A writer's originality can also be judged by the type of *similes* he or she uses. Clichéd or trite *similes* suggest a less-developed writer who is not comfortable with exploring the depths of the language, while unusual *similes* often strengthen the sentence and impress the reader. When you see a *simile*, consider the form it takes, and whether or not it strikes you as natural and flowing, rather than forced or difficult to understand.

> *Example #1:* *"The mind is like a fertile garden and fine art the seeds of wildflowers for it."* Note that the word "like" does not need to be repeated in order to sustain the *simile*.

> *Example #2:* *"He traveled quickly, as a horse with no rider would."* In this ambiguous *simile*, the reader is left to wonder if an empty horse will ride in a direct route or in a wandering manner.

Example #3: *"Your absence goes through me like thread through a needle."* What does this *simile* actually mean? Is the absence unfelt, easy to deal with, tiny, "what"? Thread is placed in the eye of the needle, and is then used to sew, so the *simile*, by itself, makes no sense.

Metaphor:

The metaphor is the window to the poet's soul.

The *metaphor* is a close relative of the *simile*—so close that at times it is difficult to tell them apart. While a *simile* compares something to another thing by pointing out how they are alike, a *metaphor* speaks of one thing as though it actually were another. Here are two sentences on the same topic, the first is a *simile*, but the second is a *metaphor*. Note the difference: *"The new boss swaggered into the office like a gunfighter in the Old West, looking for a fight"; "The new boss was Jesse James in the office looking for a fight."*

A *metaphor* speaks poetically, but it should not be viewed solely as a stylistic device. It can help your readers see something as you want them to see it—to convey not just the literal truths of a thing, but the emotional or psychological truths of it as well.

Metaphors are used to state one thing actually *is* another by using a form of the verb *to be—is, was, are, am, be,* etc.

Example #1: *"Dr. King was truly a king among men."*

Don't feel obligated to use *to be*, however, if you don't think it's necessary. If it's obvious that what you are doing is using a *metaphor*, you can skip the verb altogether and simply describe the noun:

Example #2: *"The report was released yesterday, a beacon of hope in these troubled times."*

Make sure to choose your *metaphor* carefully, being aware that the images you use could have all sorts of implications. The same general concept can be expressed in a number of ways. Let's take the sentence, *"She had a nice smile."* We could say it as,

"She had the smile of a newborn babe,"

which additionally conveys the idea of innocence. We could say it as,

"She had the smile of an angel,"

which gives it a supernatural quality and also hints at great beauty. We could say it as,

> *"She had the smile of a supermodel,"*

which also hints at great beauty, but in a more jaded, perhaps distanced, way. We could say it as,

> *"She had the smile of a Cheshire Cat,"*

which has an aura of mystery about it. There are virtually an infinite number of ways we could say the same thing, each with its own metaphorical nuances. Before committing to a *metaphor,* make sure you've thought through the different ways it will affect your reader.

Lastly, take care that your *metaphors* are obviously *metaphors.* A *metaphor* should have the illusion of truth to it, but it should always be apparent that it's an illusion. As with *hyperbole,* if your readers mistake your *metaphors* for reality, they may come away from your essay with a conclusion very different from what you intended.

> *Example #3: "A teacher has access to the most precious of commodities: the fertile soil of a young mind."*

Exercise 1:

For each of the following nouns, write two different *metaphors*. One *metaphor* should have a positive connotation while the other should have a negative connotation. Underline the *metaphor*. An example has been provided for you.

Answers will vary. Students should aim to create *metaphors* that are clearly positive or negative.

Example:
Word: snake
Positive: The road, which <u>snaked</u> into and around the mountains, was <u>a beautiful drive</u>.
Negative: <u>She is a snake</u>—sneaky, untrustworthy, and vindictive.

1. Word: **light**
    Positive:

    Negative:

2. Word: **bridge**
    Positive:

    Negative:

3. Word: **cloud**
    Positive:

    Negative:

4. Word: **freedom**
    Positive:

    Negative:

5. Word: **eye**
    Positive:

    Negative:

A good metaphor can be a breath of life for a moribund essay.

Earlier, we pointed out that a *metaphor* is similar to a *simile*, in that it compares two things or ideas, but rather than using the comparative words "like" or "as," it treats one concept as though it is literally the other. An example of this is, "*The Lord* is *my shepherd.*" Like the *simile*, the *metaphor* has many strategic uses; also, like the *simile*, the *metaphor* is the perfect vehicle for style.

Metaphors are, in many ways, the foundation of creative writing. Poetry is built upon them, fiction makes ample use of them, and even essays use them freely. By speaking of one thing as though it were something else, we not only serve a strategic end, we also break down visual barriers in the minds of our readers. A strong *metaphor* has a transformative power; it can pull a reader fully into the paper, engaging him or her on the deepest levels.

As when creating a *simile*, try to stay away from clichés. Your possibilities are virtually endless with this device, and you should feel comfortable making full use of that wide range. *Metaphor* lets you play with the English language—a language already quite playful—and you shouldn't be afraid to have some fun with it.

> *Example #1:* "*Depression is a bottomless cup that can hold no liquid.*"
>
> *Example #2:* "*The mind is a blank canvas, the writer an artist, and words his paint and brush.*"
>
> *Example #3:* "*Love is heaven, anger hell.*"

Exercise 2:

Find an example of an advertising campaign (or any public information campaign) that uses *metaphors* to inform and/or persuade. Bring visual or audio samples for the ads that you find, and explain the purpose of the *metaphors* used.

Answers will vary, but they must be valid *metaphors*, and the student must explain how the *metaphor* enhances the campaign.

Exercise 3:

Here is a list of 10 concepts, moods, or attitudes. Draw from your own background and experience, and develop a *metaphor* for each word.

The first one has been done for you as an example.

Answers will vary, but each must be a valid *metaphor* that clarifies or establishes the meaning of the abstract noun.

1. realization: *The sun rose in the back of his mind.*

2. solitude:

3. sincerity:

4. humor:

5. anticipation:

6. impatience:

7. bitter (as in taste):

8. insightful:

9. kind:

10. contempt:

The metaphor is the old sock of the rhetorical world; you wear it every day, but never pay it much attention.

Metaphor asserts that the two compared items are so close that one could actually be said to *be* the other: *"The shrill siren of his voice unnerved everyone in the office."* In this case, the voice is not similar to a shrill siren; it actually *is* that thing.

While the *metaphor* lends itself to stylistic usage, it serves a strategic purpose as well. A writer will often use a *metaphor* strategically to help you see a deeper truth about something. Rather than just describing superficial qualities or comparing it to another thing, the writer will try to jolt you into awareness by saying that the one thing is actually something different, for example, *"A mighty fortress is our God."*

Notice the two completely different values assigned, through *metaphor*, to the same trunk of old clothes found in a grandparent's attic:

> *Example #1: "That trunk of old clothes in my grandmother's attic was a gold mine of costumes for the drama club."*

> *Example #2: "That trunk of old clothes in my grandmother's attic was a morgue of fashion disasters from the past six decades."*

Simply by that one *metaphor*, you can tell that this device can be used to accomplish almost any comparison the writer might want to convey. When you come across a *metaphor*, be aware of the various strands the writer is tying together by using that specific *metaphor*. Try to determine why that exact *metaphor* was chosen, rather than any of the other options available. Think about how the *metaphor* expresses a deeper point than that made by an overt explanation. Consider what the writer is implying in each of the following:

> *Example #3: "We're not a family; we're a gathering of dysfunctional individuals who can barely interact without a fight or two breaking out."*

Example #4: "We're not a family; we're an episode of Jerry Springer looking for an audience."

Example #5: "We're not a family; we're a rich and diverse group of people who, while we might not always get along, will always pull together if any one of us needs support."

Example #6: "We're not a family, we're a well-planned machine with many parts, each with its own function, but ultimately working toward and achieving a single goal."

Notice how examples #3 and #5 are descriptions of a family, while examples #4 and #6 describe the family metaphorically.

Perhaps the best way to appreciate the power of *metaphor* is to look at a few examples of what is called a *dead metaphor*, which is an expression that once had figurative value, but the two terms are so closely related that the *metaphor* is now accepted as a literal truth.

When the drafters of the Constitution of the United States first started talking about three "branches" of government, they were metaphorically comparing the three functions of government—legislative, executive, and judicial—to the branches of a tree. The term "branches of government" has been used with great regularity, however, and a chart depicting the different aspects of government looks nearly like a graphic representation of a tree. What was once a *metaphor* has become the literal term. The same is true of the terms "branch office" and "family tree." Both were once *metaphors*, but the relationship between the depiction of a tree and a chart delineating family relationships generation by generation were so similar that the metaphoric value was eventually lost. In contrast to these dead *metaphors*, an effective *metaphor* allows the writer to understand something unfamiliar in terms of something familiar or to understand something familiar in new and refreshing terms. For example, "*All experience is an arc.*"

Metaphors are usually fairly easy to spot: If the writer seems to be saying a thing is something it obviously isn't, you're probably looking at a *metaphor*, and the larger context of the paragraph should give clues as to whether you're dealing with a *metaphor* or something else.

Exercise 4:

Make the following sentences more powerful and interesting by turning them into *metaphors*. Be sure to keep the intent of the original sentence. An example has been provided for you. *The first one has been done for you as an example.*

Answers will vary. Potential revisions/answers have been provided.

1. Sentence: Clayville is a dirty area, and the people who live there are dangerous—it should be avoided.

    Metaphor: *Stay away from Clayville—it is a cesspool and the people are infectious bacteria.*

2. Sentence: Patricia went through a long and painful delivery with her first child.

    Metaphor: **Patricia's labor, a genuine siege of Stalingrad, seemed to take forever.**

3. Sentence: The new shelter will provide food and homes to many needy families.

    Metaphor: **Unlike a mirage in a desert, the new shelter is a welcome oasis for the needy.**

4. Sentence: I couldn't understand what she was saying; the words just confused me.

    Metaphor: **Her words were a swirling vortex that knocked against the sides of my skull.**

5. Sentence: Because he didn't use any sunblock at the beach, he was badly burnt.

    Metaphor: **At the beach, he turned into a grilled tomato, red and blistered.**

6. Sentence: The storm raged violently throughout the night and damaged our home.

    Metaphor: **Last night, a fierce dragon savagely roared through our house without warning.**

The subtle, yet powerful, metaphor is the engine that drives a well-communicated thought.

Metaphor is one of the most common stylistic devices in the English language; it can bring depth, life, and illustration to works ranging from poetry to academic papers. Look at these three examples: *"Harry was a beast whenever he got the ball into his hands"*; *"The familiar is a path that you tread to avoid the unknown"*; *"Diamonds and rubies sparkled from her neck, a hummingbird at a flower."* Each one expresses a thought that is obvious, but does so figuratively, through *metaphor*. Of course, an author might have written, *"Harry ran over the tacklers whenever he got the ball into his hands,"* or *"You tend to use familiar things instead of unknown ones,"* or *"She wore diamonds and rubies,"* but the use of *metaphor* livens up the style and gives each reader a different take on the sentence. As a reader, you will encounter *metaphors* in almost everything that you read.

When you see *metaphors* used stylistically, look to see what exactly the writer is illustrating. A *metaphor* should be very carefully and deliberately chosen, not forced and unclear. *Metaphors* are used to create vivid images in the mind of the reader while also providing depth to a concept. Many *metaphors* also provide insight into the mind of the writer, and can be used to extract shades of meaning about what you are reading.

> *Example #1:* *"The world is an oyster, and education the tool with which to open it."*
>
> *Example #2:* *"I am a boat drifting upon a sea of uncertainty."*
>
> *Example #3:* *"The fire hydrants, short, squat soldiers standing at attention, reflected the afternoon sun."*

Exercise 5:

Rewrite the following statements as *metaphors*. Identify those that are rhetorical devices we have gone over (use only *hyperbole*, understatement, *litotes*, *antithesis*, *hypophora*, or *distinctio*) before changing them. Not all the phrases represent rhetorical terms that you should identify, but many do; if the statement is not a device, place an X after the type. *The first one has been done for you as an example.*

Answers for the rewritten *metaphors* will vary, but they must be valid *metaphors* and be close in meanings to the original statements.

1. Original statement: News of her winning the lottery caused no little stir in the office.
    Type of device: *Litotes*
    New metaphor: *She became a radioactive explosion when she won the lottery.*

2. Original statement: a bright smile
    Type of device: **X**
    New metaphor:

3. Original statement: Why am I so weird? Well, the apple dosen't fall too far from the tree, as they say.
    Type of device: **Hypophora**
    New metaphor:

4. Original statement: the greatest singer of all time
    Type of device: **Hyperbole**
    New metaphor:

5. Original statement: an artist who has no equal
    Type of device: **Hyperbole**
    New metaphor:

6. Original statement: day and night
    Type of device: **Antithesis**
    New metaphor:

7. Original statement: I love you more than anyone ever loved before.
    Type of device: **Hyperbole**
    New metaphor:

8. Original statement: as lovely as a spring day
    Type of device: **Simile**
    New metaphor:

9. Original statement: His personality is like a freezing rain to all those he encounters.
    Type of device: **Simile**
    New metaphor:

10. Original statement: Money's nice.
    Type of device: **Understatement**
    New metaphor:

11. Original statement: Aliens, meaning those who arrive from foreign countries, not from space, are responsible for 15% of our labor force.
    Type of device: **Distinctio**
    New metaphor:

Analogy:

The analogy is as important to the writer as the computer model is to the builder.

The *analogy* is the somewhat more down-to-earth version of the *simile*. Both compare two things for a specific purpose, but while the *simile* usually does so with a fair amount of stylistic flair, the *analogy* does so for much more pragmatic reasons. The *analogy* makes use of something already well known to explain something that is less well known. It can be one of the most effective strategic devices in both education and persuasion, helping to quickly make your reader see precisely what you mean.

Perhaps the most useful form of the *analogy* is one in which a simple argument is substituted for a more complex argument, to help your readers understand the underlying premise. Once you have them in agreement about the simple argument, it becomes much easier for them to see and accept the more complex form. The *analogy* can border on a logical fallacy when the two arguments do not actually correlate exactly, but for the most part, analogies may help to shed light on a confusing issue.

> *Example #1: "When your enemy comes to you in pain,*
> *you must do whatever is in your power*
> *to help ease that pain. For when a child*
> *comes to you in pain, do you not do*
> *everything you can? Know then that in the*
> *eyes of the Lord we are all His children."*

An *analogy* might also be used to further elaborate on a point that is already understood. Rather than substituting, the *analogy* furthers the initial point, letting the reader see aspects of it that may have been missed. It can also be used to add rhetorical force to the first point, building up the argument through stronger and stronger repetition.

> *Example #2: "The desire for wealth, when unchecked,*
> *can lead only to great evil. For though a*
> *man may begin with but a sip of wine,*
> *without restraint, the urge will grow until*
> *one day he is a drunkard, blinded to all but*
> *his need, taking whatever steps are needed*
> *to find his fix."*

> *Example #3: "As the endless waves wash eternally upon
> the shore, so does true love overwhelm the
> soul."*

Exercise 1:

Find 5 analogies used in op-ed pieces, or in advertisements, in a magazine,
or newspaper. What is the purpose of each? How effective is each? *The first
one has been done for you as an example.*

Answers will vary, but they must be valid analogies.

1. *Just as a parent is liable for damages caused by his minor children, so
   too should a dog owner be responsible for his dog.*

2.

3.

4.

5.

6.

Exercise 2:

Write 9 original analogies to evoke strong images in your readers' minds or to help them to consider a familiar idea in a new way. Be especially careful to avoid clichés and meaningless statements that, while they may technically be analogies, do nothing to help a writer achieve his or her purpose. *The first one has been done for you as an example.*

Answers will vary, but they must be valid and original analogies. Do not accept any analogies that are already in common use.

1. *Texting has become the playground note-passing of twenty-first-century kids.*

2.

3.

4.

5.

6.

7.

8.

9.

10.

Exercise 3:

In the following 5 phrases, create an *analogy* that uses each of the two elements. You may write more than one sentence to strengthen your *analogy*. *The first one has been done for you as an example.*

Answers will vary. The analogies should be logical and persuasive.

1. wealth and love
   Wealth and love are nearly the same: the more you have of either, the happier you think you are.

2. leading a sports team and leading a major corporation

3. small children and a force of nature

4. a piece of old technology and dinosaurs

5. gemstones and planets

6. intelligence and a garden

Analogies clarify and expand ideas in much the same way that pop-up greeting cards heighten the impact of the message.

While the *analogy*, the *simile*, and the *metaphor* are closely related, an *analogy* is meant to provide more information about a difficult concept by comparing it to an already understood idea. This is different from a *simile* or *metaphor*, which are used to build images in the mind of the reader. Analogies build on similarities between two ideas, comparing them to illustrate a concept. An *analogy* is a strong strategic device for writers, who use it to persuade and teach the reader.

Analogies are used by writers to quickly make a point; often by replacing a complex argument with a simpler one. An *analogy* can also be used innocently to provide definition to a concept. An example might be, *"You may think laws restricting your ability to download music from the Internet are unfair, but you wouldn't steal a CD from the music store, would you?"*

However, writers may also use two arguments that do not correlate, simply to suggest a particular conclusion to a reader, such as *"If you're going to eat fruits and vegetables grown with pesticides, you may as well throw yourself in front of a speeding truck."* When you identify an *analogy* in a text, examine the arguments used. Try to see if they are actually in agreement or if the author is trying to lead you on.

You may also find an *analogy* used to add emphasis to an argument. The point may be clearly understood, but the *analogy* adds depth to the concept, or it enforces the point being argued. Examine the *analogy* closely to see how the author builds on an existing argument by tying several concepts together.

> *Example # 1:* *"Those who oppose abortion and cite the right to life must also oppose the death penalty in the name of the same right. To say that euthanasia takes the decision of life and death out of God's hands and puts it into human hands is to admit that the artificial extension of life is likewise tantamount to playing God."*

Exercise 4:

Choose the letter of the phrase that best completes the *analogy*. Then, in a short sentence, explain the author's meaning. For each *analogy*, two answers are better than the other two, so you need to explain why you chose the one you did. You should also explain why the two that aren't good analogies do not work. *The first one has been done for you as an example.*

1. **The physics class was so tedious and confusing that it reminded the freshmen of _____.**

   A. watching a baby bird learn to fly
   B. reading a mystery novel that doesn't reveal the killer until the end
   C. watching a foreign movie with no subtitles
   D. witnessing a nuclear explosion

The physics class would be hard to understand and will take a long time to complete.

   A. *While learning to fly is a difficult task, the experience of watching a bird learn to fly is neither confusing nor boring. Therefore, this analogy works, but only partially. C is the better answer.*
   B. *Reading a suspenseful mystery novel may, like a physics class, be an intellectually rigorous activity. However, the physics class is described as wearisome, while a suspenseful novel is generally engaging.*
   C. *Both the foreign film and the physics class may be difficult to understand and, as a result, may be hard to sit through. Hence, this is the best answer.*
   D. *Witnessing a nuclear explosion would be shocking, distressing, and difficult. However, it would by no means be tedious or confusing.*

2. The jacket was so tight that it limited the movement of her arms. When she tried to get it off, she looked like _____.
    A. a sea turtle gliding through the ocean
    B. a tyrannosaurus rex trying to pick up something
    C. an angry protestor waving a sign
    D. a duck flapping its wings

A tight jacket restricts movement and makes removing it difficult. Those who have experienced or witnessed this can attest that it is slightly comedic.

A. The opposite is shown here—gliding rather than struggling.

B. Because a t-rex has short arms, it has limited movement, similar to what the girl has in the restrictive jacket.

C. No similarities.

D. When someone tries to remove a tight jacket, the person might flap his or her arms like a bird while trying to take it off. This is the second-best answer.

3. Animals have feelings, so killing animals just for their fur _____.
    A. is similar to killing a deer only for its antlers
    B. is morally wrong and should be illegal
    C. is like destroying a rainforest to make paper
    D. is just as heinous as the experiments the Nazis performed on victims in concentration camps

Killing an animal for its fur is arguably wasteful and cruel.

A. This makes an accurate comparison and works better than the others.

B. This is just an opinion.

C. Those who destroy rainforests do not consider the animals and/or people who inhabit them, but the comparison in A is closer.

D. The Nazis didn't consider the lives of those they experimented on, but this *analogy* is too melodramatic.

4. Management's refusal to accept the union's concession _____.

    A. came as a surprise
    B. made me think of a spoiled child insulting an expensive gift he'd just opened
    C. made it seem as if they wanted to prolong the strike
    D. was exactly what happened in the nurses' strike last year

    a. Not an *analogy*

    b. This is the best choice. The speaker is comparing management's behavior in the strike to the way a child acts when the gift—however nice—is not *exactly* what the child wants.

    c. Not an *analogy*

    d. This compares the current situation with another, almost identical one. Because they are so similar, however, the comparison cannot be said to be an *analogy*.

5. I took a long look at the ancient gold prospector and noticed that the wrinkles on his face _____.
    A. are as defined and deep as the ridges of the Grand Canyon
    B. cascade like a waterfall
    C. tell the story of his hardships
    D. make me think of a bag of old fruit

    The prospector's face reflects his life.

    A. The *analogy* is a clear comparison between the man's face and the canyon; it is slightly more appropriate than (C) because it has the flavor of the man's life in it.

    B. Wrinkles do not move like waterfalls do.

    C. This is not an analogy.

    D. A bag of wrinkled fruit conveys the idea that the man is old. However, the canyon (A) is a more appropriate analogy for an "ancient gold prospector."

6. These glasses, which I never wanted to wear in the first place,
    _____.
    A. make me stand out too much in school, and I won't wear them
    B. are so good at distances that it seems as if I'm wearing binoculars
    C. simply do not help, probably because the prescription is wrong
    D. are now as essential to my life as an old friend

The glasses had been disliked, but now seem to have a positive aspect to them.

A. **Just a sentence, not an *analogy***

B. **The *analogy*, which includes *hyperbole*, is a great comparison. It would depend on the context of the rest of the paragraph, however, to determine whether this *analogy* is more fitting than (D).**

C. **Not an *analogy***

D. **This comparison between seeing well and loving someone states the relationship in terms anyone can understand.**

Device #12

Allusion:

You don't have to be Holden Caulfield to appreciate a good allusion.

An *allusion* is a reference to some fairly well-known event, place, or person: *"This new war was Vietnam all over again."* Unlike a detailed comparison or reference, an *allusion* is short and usually not formally introduced. The new war, according to the *analogy*, must be a drawn-out, difficult one that involves protests by Americans and many soldiers' deaths. *Allusions* can be used to help your reader see a broader picture, to evoke a negative or positive feeling, or to add credibility to your writing.

Used in a weak or inconclusive manner, however, *allusions* can cause problems: *"This painting resembles Medusa."* Knowing that the *allusion* refers to a monster from Greek mythology with hair like snakes, who could turn a person into stones does not help the reader in understanding what the painting looks like because there are many possibilities for individual interpretation: Is it a painting of snakes, of the actual monster, of something that looks like a monster, or what?

Like an *analogy*, an *allusion* can also be used as a shortcut to help your reader understand what you're talking about. Rather than describing the concept in great detail, you can compare it to something well known in the general culture, as in *"He hammered the ball the way Babe Ruth did."* This gives your reader something to relate to, without your having to spell it out. By choosing *allusions* that have a certain type of association, you can evoke a specific emotion in your reader as well. *Allusions* to happy historical events or stories will improve your reader's regard for whatever you're talking about, while an *allusion* to a historical atrocity will lend a darker cast.

While anything sufficiently well known can be alluded to, there are a number of sources that work particularly well. Shakespeare, classical mythology, and the Bible are all virtually limitless repositories of wonderful ideas that can be used for *allusion*. Characters, story lines, and events in these works tend to encompass a single concept or set of concepts which your *allusion* will draw upon. Many *allusions* have been used so commonly they have become accepted terms—examples include an Achilles heel or a Trojan horse.

When using *allusions*, keep your target audience in mind. While referencing lesser Greek gods and heroes might be perfectly suitable for older students, it might not work as well for younger ones. Similarly, alluding to popular culture may now seem like a good idea, but it will tie your essay to a limited era, and may not be understood by those out of touch with contemporary television or media.

Example #1: *"Scientists have reached further and further to unlock the secrets of the universe. But there are those who would argue that like Icarus, science ignores the ever-nearing sun at its own peril."* (an *allusion* to the Greek myth in which Icarus, on wings made by his father, flies too close to the sun, and perishes)

Example #2: *"These tribes survive and even thrive, in spite of the fact that, like the lilies in the field, they toil not."* (an *allusion* to the Gospel of Matthew, chapter 6, verse 28: "Consider the lilies of the field, how they grow; they toil not, neither do they spin.")

Example #3: *"The giant squid, at lengths of over 40 feet, are true Leviathans of the underwater world."* (an *allusion* to an enormous sea creature mentioned several times in the Old Testament and usually taken to be a demon or a symbol of the devil)

Exercise 1:

Identify the following *allusions* and state what each is meant to convey. Then, write a sentence that uses the *allusion* properly. *The first one has been done for you as an example.*

For these exercises, answers will vary, but they must be plausible *allusions*, and students must provide a reasonable explanation of how the *allusion* clarifies the term.

1. Allusion: The Twelve Labors of Hercules
   Explanation: Devised as a punishment for Hercules, the 12 tasks were difficult and thought to be nearly impossible.
   Sentence: While the jobs Harold's boss gave him weren't the Twelve Labors of Hercules, they certainly were challenging.

From the Bible
2.   Allusion: Job
     Explanation:

     Sentence:

3.   Allusion: Samson and Delilah
     Explanation:

     Sentence:

From Greek Mythology
4.   Allusion: Pandora
     Explanation:

     Sentence:

5.   Allusion: The Oracle at Delphi
     Explanation:

     Sentence:

6.   Allusion: Atlas
     Explanation:

     Sentence:

From Popular Culture
7.   Allusion: Bill Gates
     Explanation:

     Sentence:

8. Allusion: Homer Simpson
    Explanation:

    Sentence:

9. Allusion: Muhammad Ali
    Explanation:

    Sentence:

Exercise 2:

Use 5 original *allusions* in sentences that evoke strong images or show
a familiar idea in a new way. Be especially careful to avoid clichés and
meaningless statements that, while they may technically be *allusions*, would
do nothing to help a writer achieve his or her purpose or to help a reader
understand the *allusions*. *The first one has been done for you as an example.*

Answers will vary.

1. *While you might think that owning your first car might make you feel
    like Perseus riding his winged horse, if you're not careful, you find
    yourself chained to a rock like Prometheus.*

2.

3.

4.

5.

6.

Good allusions can give your writing the beauty of Helen and the power of Achilles.

An *allusion*, being a reference to a person, place, or event, cannot be effective unless it is one that the reader is likely to understand. We talked earlier about the strategic value *allusions* can have in helping your reader to understand something quickly and easily. They are also great stylistic devices because they allow you to interject a completely different feel into your writing instantly, as in the following example, *"The meeting seemed never to end; it was Zeus's eagle nibbling away forever at my liver."*

In areas where your writing seems to be lagging a bit, *allusions* can make things more pertinent. In the middle of a list that is beginning to feel boring, you can throw in an *allusion* to an exciting event or person, which will change the mood right away. Think of *allusions* not only as strategic devices to help explain something to your reader, but also as an easily accessible spice you can shake in wherever it's needed.

As in other uses of the *allusion*, take care that the one you choose is recognizable to your reader. While it's less important in a purely stylistic context that readers understand exactly why you're making the comparison, it is probably a good idea that they at least recognize the name or event. At the same time, plenty of writers do make use of *allusions* that sound good and that their readers will only barely know. Greek mythology, for example, is sprinkled throughout writing aimed at readers who probably don't have a comprehensive knowledge of the myths—but even if they don't know exactly who Perseus was, or what the Twelve Labors of Hercules were, the names will still resonate, and context should let them get what they need to know.

> *Example #1:* *"He held the trophy aloft like Perseus holding the Gorgon's head."*

> *Example #2:* *"There was no burning bush, but he acted as though the instructions came from on high."*

> *Example #3:* *"He delivered the line as if he were playing Hamlet for Shakespeare himself."*

Exercise 3:

Cartoons like *The Simpsons* and situation comedies on TV often employ *allusions* for caustic wit and humor that are more sophisticated than slapstick. Watch an episode of one of these types of shows (or any other in which you are likely to hear characters allude to history, literature, current events, popular culture, etc.). Identify at least 3 *allusions*, and explain the effect and significance of each. *The first one has been done for you as an example.*

Answers will vary, but they must be valid *allusions*, and the students must cite their sources, evaluate their effectiveness, and explain how each enhances the meaning of the text.

1. Allusion: *"It was like Romeo and Juliet, only it ended in tragedy."*

    Source: *The Simpsons*

    Effect: *Comic because Romeo and Juliet was a tragedy.*

    Significance: *Romeo and Juliet is a classic, tragic love story, and Milhouse is implying that his first love was like that.*

2. Allusion:

    Source:

    Effect:

    Significance:

3. Allusion:

    Source:

    Effect:

    Significance:

4. Allusion:

    Source:

    Effect:

    Significance:

Exercise 4:

Write a sentence that alludes to each of the following people. If you are completely unfamiliar with the name, look the person up on the Internet or in an encyclopedia. Be sure that readers would be able to identify the *allusion*. Choose one aspect of the figure to focus on.

Answers will vary. *Allusion*s should be clear and accurate.

1. Cupid:

2. Pocahontas:

3. Martin Luther King, Jr.:

4. Scrooge:

5. Mother Teresa:

Device #13   ***Eponym:***

Keep moving through these devices, and
soon you'll be a regular Hemingway.

An *eponym* is similar to an *allusion,* referring to a specific famous person to link his or her attributes with someone else. Using an *eponym* well can be something of a balancing act; if the person is too obscure, no one will understand your reference, but if it's too well known, it may come across as a cliché. Note the difference between these two *eponyms.* The first is easily recognizable, but the second is obscure and would be understood only by someone in the field of Hindu medicine: *"Gary was an Abe Lincoln in yesterday's debate"; "Agnivesha would have been proud of the patient's recovery." Eponyms* should be used sparingly, but with the right touch they can give a perfect finish to a piece.

There are a number of *eponyms* that are used very frequently. You've no doubt run into them many times in your reading and have probably used them on more than one occasion. We might call a man whom we want to label as clutching tightly to his money a Scrooge. A person with strength beyond that of normal men might be labeled a Hercules. Then, of course there's Einstein, whose name has become synonymous with (or eponymous for) intellectual brilliance.

Although any famous person or character can be used as an *eponym*, be certain the person you use is well known for whatever attribute you want to link to your target. For example, while Nero might have been a patron of the arts, it is his decadence and arrogance that is most closely associated with his name. While Stalin was undoubtedly a cunning general, it is his stony demeanor and vicious method of dealing with dissent that we remember when we hear his name. In some cases, you may feel that the exact trait you're trying to convey isn't immediately obvious. If that's the case, you can elaborate on the person to make it clear why you're making the comparison—for example saying, *"He had the strength of Hercules,"* rather than simply, *"He was a Hercules."*

> *Example #1: "A modern day Moses, he led his nation to
> a new beginning."*

> *Example #2: "The senator, with the patience of Job,
> endured setback after setback, until his
> time finally came."*

> *Example #3:* "No one expected our second-rate team to
> win that game, but no one knew our secret
> weapon. He was our Prometheus, snatching
> fire from the gods that we might triumph."

Exercise 1:

Explain the point that an author expects the reader to make through each of
the following *eponyms. The first one has been done for you as an example.*

**Answers will vary. Some students may not be familiar with some
of the figures, which should emphasize to them that *eponyms*
need to be relevant to and understood by the reader.**

1. Shakespeare: *Famous writer of plays; symbol of Elizabethan England*

2. Benedict Arnold: **betrayer of one's country**

3. Queen Victoria: **long reign; beloved monarch; grieving widow**

4. Josef Stalin: **extreme cruelty; personal betrayal of a cause**

5. Ronald Reagan: **popular leader**

6. Jezebel: **feminine betrayal; temptress**

7. Robert Kennedy: **popular politician; "cursed family"; killed
   when young**

8. Marilyn Monroe: **legendary beauty; tragic figure**

9. Abraham Lincoln: **wise and just leader**

10. Albert Einstein: **scientific innovator and genius**

11. Rocky Balboa: **perseverance; unlikely winner**

Exercise 2:

Now, write 10 sentences with original *eponyms*. Be especially careful to avoid clichés and meaningless statements that, while they may technically be *eponyms*, would do nothing to help a reader understand the connection or a writer achieve his or her purpose. *The first one has been done for you as an example.*

Answers will vary, but they must be plausible and original *eponyms.*

1. The kids in the neighborhood consider the old man a regular Santa Claus. Readers will immediately understand that the old man is kind and pleasant; maybe he gives out gifts to children at Christmas, and he might be short and round with a white beard.

2.

3.

4.

5.

6.

7.

8.

9.

10.

11.

With care and a little effort, even your school's Forrest Gump can become its Faulkner.

Like the *allusion*, the *eponym* has a great deal of strategic value, but can also serve equally well as a stylistic device. *Eponyms* can be added to spice up an otherwise banal description, though they probably should not be used as liberally as *allusions*. An *eponym* is ideal to transform a description of some mundane person (perhaps a middle-of-the-road government accountant) into something with more punch (a Sisyphus, laboring under the endless weight of government paperwork).

As with *allusions*, *eponyms* chosen for stylistic reasons have a bit more leeway than those being used strategically. The person you reference doesn't need to immediately bring to mind a long list of qualities and accomplishments. Names should be recognizable to the majority of your readers, however, and ideally, they'll know something about what the person is known for. Therefore, referring to someone in your class in a paper that would be read by people in another city is not a sensible idea.

> *Example #1:* *"She ran around frantically, Alice chasing the rabbit."*

> *Example #2:* *"The way he talked, you'd think he was Atlas holding up the heavens."*

> *Example #3:* *"This modern-day da Vinci has a long list of amazing accomplishments."*

Exercise 3:

Over the next week or so, pay attention to the newspapers, magazines, or blogs that you read. Listen closely to people you hear speaking, whether on television, radio, online, or in person. Note any *eponyms* you read or hear and list them. Also, decide whether each particular use is effective or not and explain why. *The first one has been done for you as an example.*

Answers will vary, but they must be valid *eponyms*, and the students must cite their sources, evaluate their effectiveness, and explain how each specific *eponym* enhances the meaning, tone, or mood of the text.

1. Eponym: *"...an artist of the Banal, the Einstein of the mediocre..."*
   Source: **St. George and the Godfather,** *by Norman Mailer*
   Effective or not: *very effective*
   Explanation: *Everyone knows Einstein to be brilliant, so this eponym clearly suggests that Nixon was brilliantly mediocre.*

2. Eponym:
   Source:
   Effective or not:
   Explanation:

3. Eponym:
   Source:
   Effective or not:
   Explanation:

4. Eponym:
   Source:
   Effective or not:
   Explanation:

5.   Eponym:
     Source:
     Effective or not:
     Explanation:

6.   Eponym:
     Source:
     Effective or not:
     Explanation:

7.   Eponym:
     Source:
     Effective or not:
     Explanation:

8.   Eponym:
     Source:
     Effective or not:
     Explanation:

9.   Eponym:
     Source:
     Effective or not:
     Explanation:

10. Eponym:
     Source:
     Effective or not:
     Explanation:

Exercise 4:

Write a sentence that uses an *eponym* for each of the following people. Be sure that readers would be able to identify him or her based on the context you provide. *The first one has been done for you as an example.*

Answers will vary. *Eponyms* should be clear and accurate.

1. **Sherlock Holmes:** *When we played "Clue," Kanye was a regular Sherlock Holmes; he won every game.*

2. Venus:

3. Pablo Picasso:

4. Indiana Jones:

5. Attila the Hun:

6. Mahatma Gandhi:

Soon you'll know enough rhetoric to be a regular Cicero.

"No one wants Bart Simpson to be in charge of his or her fate." *Eponyms* usually involve well-known characters so that the intent of the comparison is clear; Hitler, for example, might be used to illustrate a particular level of evil. Obscure figures might be used in specific contexts, but only if the writer knows that the audience will understand the reference.

When a writer uses an *eponym*, it is often to describe a character or clarify some aspect of the character's personality. If a writer describes an individual as a Grinch, for example, you might infer that the character being described is unfriendly and misanthropic. If an *eponym* is not descriptive enough, a writer might add a qualifier, saying, for example, *"Albert's shortness rivaled Napoleon's,"* rather than simply referring to Albert as "a Napoleon." If the *eponym* does not immediately convey the character trait desired, it suggests that the writer may be writing for a limited audience, or may have chosen a poor *eponym*.

Example #1: *"We call Manuel 'the Churchill of the art department' because of the way he inspires us to press on, even during difficult times."*

Example #2: *"I love serving on committees with Michelle. When it comes to making the company money, she's a regular Midas."*

Example #3: *"It's not Shakespeare, but I think it will be sufficient for a biology report."*

Device #14   ***Sententia:***

A word to the wise is sufficient.

Sententia is simply a fancy term for a quotation, maxim, or wise saying. Usually *sententia* makes use of general maxims that aren't attributed to a single source, but it may also be used to quote a real person, although this use is less common.

Sententia is best used to sum up what you've been talking about in the preceding paragraphs. A strong *sententia* seems familiar, obvious, and often witty. It adds the weight of centuries of belief to your argument or discussion topic, making it much harder for your reader to ignore.

Take care, however, not to oversimplify concepts you have built up as complex and full of nuance. *Sententia* is most effective when its short, succinct wisdom seems to tie together everything that came before it. If you read your finished paper, and the *sententia* seems to shrug aside your earlier points rather than validate them, rethink its use.

People love pithy statements, and summing up your argument with a sound bite helps ensure they'll remember your broader point. By choosing maxims or quotations which are familiar to readers, you also set up your argument as established wisdom. In combination, this one-two punch helps your essay deliver a knockout blow.

> *Example #1: "As is often said, a bird in the hand is worth two in the bush."*

> *Example #2: "We would do well to remember, however, that all is fair in love and war."*

> *Example #3: "As Epictetus wisely noted, 'no great thing is created suddenly.'"*

Exercise 1:

The following are maxims from Benjamin Franklin's *Poor Richard's Almanack*. Select 10 of these statements. What point are they making? How effective are they?

1. There are no gains without pains.
   Everything has a cost; nothing comes without some effort or loss.

2. At the workingman's house hunger looks in but dares not enter.
   As long as a person is working, there might not be a *lot* of money for food, but there will be food to eat.

3. Industry pays debts while despair increases them.
   Industry here means the willingness to work hard, ambition. The adage says that a willingness to work earns money and pays off debts while a lack of hope, and, thus, the absence of the will to work, drives the despairing person even deeper into debt.

4. Diligence is the mother of good luck.
   There really is no such thing as "luck." Those "lucky" ones, who have good things, actually have them because of their hard work and attention to detail.

5. God gives all things to industry.
   Again, industry means the willingness to work hard. Franklin is saying that God rewards those who are willing to work hard.

6. Plough deep while sluggards sleep and you shall have corn to sell and to keep.
   The farmer is working hard while the lazy person is sleeping. Eventually, the farmer will have a harvest to feed himself and to sell for cash (i.e., prosperity).

7. Work while it is called today for you know not how much you may be hindered tomorrow.
   Do not put anything off until tomorrow because you do not know what events might transpire to prevent you from completing what you *could have done* today.

8. One today is worth two tomorrows.
   Today is more or less a certainty, so get done what you can. Tomorrow is completely uncertain.

9. Light purse? Heavy heart.
   Poverty causes pain and worry.

10. If you were a servant would you not be ashamed that a good master should catch you idle? Then if you are your own master be ashamed to catch yourself idle.
    A servant would want to *please* a "good" master with hard work. Therefore, if you are your own master, please yourself with hard work.

11. Trouble springs from idleness and grievous toil from needless ease.
    Being lazy and idle breeds troubles and, in the end, causes more work than keeping yourself legitimately busy.

12. Industry gives comfort and plenty and respect.
    Keeping busy will make you wealthy, and people will respect you.

13. Keep thy shop and thy shop will keep thee.
    Pay attention to your business and you will have a strong source of income.

14. If you would have your business done, go; if not, send.
    If you want something done right, do it yourself. If you want it done poorly, send someone else to do it for you.

15. Women and wine, game and deceit make the wealth small and the wants great.
    Living life in the "fast lane," a life of "celebrity," will exhaust your fortune and leave you in poverty.

16. Many estates are spent in the getting,
    Since women for tea forsook spinning and knitting,
    And men for punch forsook hewing and splitting.
    When men and women stopped working and started living "social lives," the fortunes that their hardworking ancestors had amassed dwindled away.

17. What maintains one vice would bring up two children.
    Bad habits like drinking, smoking, and gambling are expensive.

18. Fools make feasts and wise men eat them.
    Foolish people squander their efforts, while wise people benefit from them.

Exercise 2:

Now, write 5 original *sententia* that evoke strong images in your readers' minds or help them to consider a familiar idea in a new way. Be especially careful to avoid clichés and meaningless statements that, while they may technically be *sententia*, would do nothing to help a writer achieve his or her purpose. Since these statements have no authentic context, we won't worry about whether or not they are effective, though that *will*, of course be a concern when you use *sententia* in your writing. *The first one has been done for you as an example.*

Answers will vary, but they must be valid *sententia*.

1. *You can't plant a tree without digging a hole.*

2.

3.

4.

5.

Write appropriately for your audience, and do not cast your pearls before swine.

   Sententia is the rhetorical device most commonly used to illustrate and sum up a point. Usually, authors will use maxims that have entered common usage and have no defined source. In other cases, a specific person, such as Benjamin Franklin or Abraham Lincoln, may be quoted. Authors choose *sententia* with care, looking for strong sayings that add authority to the idea being discussed.

Authors rely on the established expertise, as presented by *sententia*, to elegantly tie up the loose ends of an argument. In other words, *sententia* allows writers to say what they want to say by using another's words to express the sentiment well. In some cases, a well-chosen *sententia* may serve as a witty and clear summation, subtly showing that another person agrees with the author's point and emphasizing the point at the same time.

> *Example #1: "After all, Rome was not built in a day."*
> This maxim might summarize a politician's argument as to why a highway project has not been completed.

In other cases, an author may choose a poor *sententia* which actually undermines the point by dismissing the arguments previously laid out.

> *Example #2: "Our protagonist was a kind man and remembered that revenge is a dish best served cold."* A writer using this *sententia* to bolster the concept that a mistake should be forgiven has, in fact, made the opposite argument.

Readers should be wary of *sententia* because it is sometimes used to prop up a weak or faulty argument. When you spot an author using a clever saying to sum up or support an argument, carefully examine whatever factual and authoritative support the author has provided, and then ask yourself what is meant by using that particular saying.

> *Example #3: "It does no good to wonder what could have been, when you could bloom where you are planted."* Is this intended to emphasize that a person can flourish anywhere, or does it mean thinking about the past is useless, or, possibly, that people's perceptions are tinted by their backgrounds?

Exercise 3:

Complete the adages that follow by filling in the blank with the appropriate ending. The first one has been done for you as an example. You must be careful with phrases that are too familiar, or you might be marked down for using clichés. In addition, do not use them frequently, or it could cause a problem.

1.	As you sow,	__J__	A.	to catch a trout.
2.	Barking dogs	_____	B.	after the event.
3.	Children should	_____	C.	before you have it.
4.	Desires are	_____	D.	seldom bite.
5.	You must lose a fly	_____	E.	where the shoe pinches.
6.	Happy is the country	_____	F.	has many friends.
7.	It is easy to be wise	_____	G.	make light work.
8.	Knowledge	_____	H.	that has no history.
9.	Lend your money and	_____	I.	nourished by delays.
10.	Many hands	_____	J.	so shall you reap.
11.	Never spend your money	_____	K.	be seen and not heard.
12.	Only the wearer knows	_____	L.	that wears a crown.
13.	Success	_____	M.	lose your friend.
14.	Uneasy lies the head	_____	N.	is power.

1. (J) **As you sow, so shall you reap.**
2. (D) **Barking dogs seldom bite.**
3. (K) **Children should be seen and not heard.**
4. (I) **Desires are nourished by delays.**
5. (A) **You must lose a fly to catch a trout.**
6. (H) **Happy is the country that has no history.**
7. (B) **It is easy to be wise after the event.**
8. (N) **Knowledge is power.**
9. (M) **Lend your money and lose your friend.**
10. (G) **Many hands make light work.**
11. (C) **Never spend your money before you have it.**
12. (E) **Only the wearer knows where the shoe pinches.**
13. (F) **Success has many friends.**
14. (L) **Uneasy lies the head that wears a crown.**

Device #15   ***Exemplum:***

You'll find this device to be very useful, especially in research papers, for example, when you want to cite specific authorities or quote specific sources.

Exemplum is one of the most often used rhetorical devices, and one you've probably never thought of as a special device. As the name suggests, it is simply providing your reader with an example to illustrate your point: "*The U.S. government gives its citizens freedom; one illustration of this is that we have the right to criticize our leaders.*" *Exemplum* is a key part of any essay, and it should be a major part of your writing strategy.

Some of the strongest examples you can give to illustrate a point or make a case for your argument are examples drawn from the real world. If you can come up with a good historical event that serves your purpose, it will nearly always strengthen your essay. Take care, however, to make sure that you have used correct facts. Since you won't have notes while taking standardized exams, you will most likely want to stick to broader examples that stay away from exact dates or places. Of course, if you happen to have that information at your fingertips and are certain it is accurate, by all means use it.

More likely, though, you will be using *exemplum* that you come up with on your own. It is entirely acceptable to use fictional examples in your essays, so long as you don't present them as fact. When coming up with examples to fit your situation, keep an eye towards their plausibility. An example that seems completely unrealistic will do more harm than good, as shown here: "*America should never intervene in foreign affairs; after all, we lost over 100,000 soldiers during WWII.*"

A good *exemplum* should support the point you are trying to make in a way that seems natural. An *exemplum* can also serve to make more nuanced points, in addition to the primary one. Make use of the fact that readers will respond to actual examples more openly than to direct argument; *exemplum* is a wonderful way to broach points that might be too contentious for the main thrust of your essay.

> *Example #1:* "*An example can be seen in the Seattle general strike of 1919, when for five days more than sixty housand workers ground the city to a halt.*" Obviously, this *exemplum* relates to previous information.

Example #2: "To see the truth in this we need look no
further than the daily television news, in
which a single segment lasting for more
than five minutes is the rare exception."
This contains no reference to an actual
example, yet the example is apparent in
the statement.

Example #3: "Let us consider a woman born
into poverty; let us see that she has
no opportunity for education, no
encouragement from her parents, and no
financial resources to fall back on. Can we
truly contend the choices open to her in
life are equal to a man's?" Note how the
exemplum here is at the beginning of the
comment.

Exercise 1:

For each of the following topics, list 3 *exemplum* that support the
statement. *The first one has been done for you as an example.*
**Answers will vary, but they should all provide accurate examples
that support the original statement.**

1. **Sports heroes should not be models that children should emulate.**
    A. *Sports figures have become increasingly more disrespectful of each
        other and of the public in general.*
    B. *Salaries for professional athletes have created a financial separation
        between them and the general public.*
    C. *Many athletes have nothing to fall back upon once their careers have
        ended.*

2. **The U.S. is a force that should police the rest of the world.**
    A.

    B.

    C.

3. Racism is an economic problem, not a social one.

    A.

    B.

    C.

4. Those who have a good education will ultimately make more money.

    A.

    B.

    C.

5. Censorship is beneficial/detrimental to society. (Choose one.)

    A.

    B.

    C.

6. Exercise improves one's overall health.

    A.

    B.

    C.

Most rhetorical devices, for instance the exemplum, help the writer communicate with the reader.

The *exemplum* is probably the most-used rhetorical device, as it illustrates or clarifies a point: *"I believe Wilt Chamberlain is the greatest player in NBA history. For instance, he scored 100 points in a single game and played nearly every minute of every game."* Good examples are used to build strong arguments, and readers should pay close attention to them. An *exemplum* can often be spotted by phrases such as "for example," or "for instance," which serve as flags for the reader, but *exemplum* may also be disguised and may be missing the key phrases.

In some cases, writers may invent an *exemplum* to support a point. In this case, they will usually use life experience and knowledge to illustrate a situation. This type of *exemplum* can usually be easily identified, and a careful writer will have constructed a believable and convincing example. When you encounter this type of *exemplum*, consider it carefully to determine whether it is plausible and supports the writer's argument.

In other instances, writers use examples from history or literature to make a point. When a writer cites an historical event as an example, readers should take note. It is always worthwhile to check the facts to make sure that the example being used actually supports the writer's argument and is being presented accurately and without bias.

An *exemplum* may also be used to introduce information that might be argumentative or questionable, or to make additional supportive points. As a reader, you should be wary of examples because they sometimes tend to have more persuasive power than does a direct argument. When writers introduce an example, consider what sort of point they are making or supporting with the example and what response they are attempting to evoke.

> *Example #1:* *"People are often attracted to things which are forbidden to them. During the 1920s, for example, Prohibition in the United States caused illicit alcohol sales to skyrocket."*

> *Example #2:* *"As anyone who has ridden public transit knows, graffiti has no limits on what is said or restrictions on where it can be found."*

Example #3: *"Alcohol-related fatalities tend to be lower in areas that use law enforcement checkpoints to identify drunk drivers, just to offer one example."*

One final issue to consider when evaluating a writer's use of *exemplum* is the number of examples offered. Granted, time and space constraints might limit the writer's ability to list example after example, and you certainly don't need to read more than a few pertinent ones to begin to see the writer's point, but as the adage says, *"One swallow doth not a spring make."* In other words, the fact that the writer is able and willing to provide a single example does not necessarily mean the general point is valid.

Exercise 2:

From the 5 arguments that follow, identify the 2 in which the *exemplum* provides little or no support for the argument.

1. Technology has increased the speed of communication. The cellular phone has made it much easier to reach someone and have a conversation.

2. There are many violent movies that lead their young viewers to be desensitized towards violence. The movie *Home Alone* shows a young boy using a house full of dangerous traps to catch two bumbling burglars.

3. The party will be well supervised. There will be eight adults present, and all of them are parents of people who were invited.

4. Wind power is one example of a way that the United States can escape the dominance of oil. For example, in Pennsylvania, coal mining has tripled since the conflict began. **The fact that coal mining has tripled has no bearing whatsoever on the issue of wind power.**

5. This has been the rainiest spring I can remember. Last spring, my water bills were three times what they have been this year. **Without explaining that the individual had to water his or her plants and lawn last year, the connection between rainfall and water bill is not apparent.**

Exercise 3:

From the same 5 arguments in Exercise 1, choose the 2 that are *best* supported by the examples.

1. Technology has increased the speed of communication. The cellular phone has made it much easier to reach someone and have a conversation.
   Here, the assertion that technology has sped communication is immediately followed by the accurate and relevant example of the cellular phone.

2. There are many violent movies that lead their young viewers to be desensitized towards violence. The movie *Home Alone* shows a young boy using a house full of dangerous traps to catch two bumbling burglars.
   A reader may disagree with the example, but the author does provide one—by name—of the type of movie he or she is criticizing.

3. The party will be well supervised. There will be eight adults present, and all of them are parents of people who were invited.

4. Wind power is one example of a way that the United States can escape the dominance of oil. For example, in Pennsylvania, coal mining has tripled since the conflict began.

5. This has been the rainiest spring I can remember. Last spring, my water bills were three times what they have been this year.

Exercise 4:

Provide an *exemplum* to support each of these 3 unsupported arguments.
Answers will vary, but the examples must include the points introduced in the statement and support, not contradict, them.

1. Reality television shows are far superior to silly situation comedies.

2. It is very easy to go from being a comic to being a serious actor.

3. The legal driving age should be raised to twenty-five.

ORGANIZATION

Device #16   ***Climax:***

From concept, to plan, to fully developed paper…

Building to a *climax* is a way of organizing ideas in your writing so that they proceed from the least to the most important. It is one of the basic principles of structure—you slowly build your reader up to a state of excitement, then deliver your crowning statements.

Anything can be ordered climactically: from single words, to short clauses, to longer sentences, to entire paragraphs in a paper. You may list items based on the relative emphasis you want them to have, the scope they cover, or the importance in a general sense. A *climax* will usually make use of parallelism as well, to help drive home the build-up of ideas. By keeping the general form the same, it is obvious to your readers that they are seeing things in progression, rather than just a list of individual items.

Take care that the beginning point in a paper is sufficiently interesting to make your reader want to continue reading. It will not serve you well to begin too far down the ladder of importance, so that your reader is yawning as soon as the reading has begun. Ideally, you want your reader to be drawn in immediately and dragged along, enthralled until the ultimate *climax*.

> *Example #1:* "*He began his career writing horoscopes for a local paper. By nineteen, he was writing front-page stories. At twenty-two, he published his first collection of short essays. And just nine days shy of his twenty-sixth birthday, he won the Pulitzer for his work at* the New York Times.*"*

> *Example #2:* "*Caution can be a useful human emotion. Fear tends to cloud our better judgment. Anger turns us away from what we know to be right. Hate overwhelms us and ultimately devours our humanity.*"

> *Example #3:* "*Curiosity leads to discovery, leads to knowledge, leads to wisdom.*"

Exercise 1:

Write 10 original constructions that build to a *climax*. Be especially careful to avoid clichés and meaningless statements that, while they may technically employ *climax*, would do nothing to help a writer achieve the intended purpose.

Answers will vary, but they must be valid and original series, and each must build to a *climax*.

1.

2.

3.

4.

5.

6.

7.

8.

9.

10.

Start with an idea, gather information, and take the appropriate action.

The core of organized writing lies in the *climax*, the culminating point in a sequence of ideas, ordered from least to most important. This order begins with an interesting point to draw the reader in, and ends with a grand finale designed to drive a point or idea home. This organizational structure appears at every level, from individual sentences *("He won the face-off, took the puck over the line on a breakaway, and drove the shot into the net to score the game-winning goal.")* to an entire written work.

The *climax* should be very distinctive and clear to you as a reader. If the *climax* seems somewhat obscured, it suggests that the writer did not organize ideas well. On the other hand, if the sequence seems somehow "off" to you, perhaps the writer is trying to highlight what is considered to be the climactic point. Look to the *climax* of an argument to sum up the points a writer makes and to deliver a final message to you as a reader. The points along the way should not be dull, either; as a reader, you should be drawn in and captivated by the sequence of ideas or events.

> *Example #1:* *"Baking bread begins with proofing the yeast. Then the baker adds oil, salt, and flour, mixing the ingredients evenly and carefully. After twenty minutes of kneading, the bread is set aside to rise. Finally, the bread is baked in the oven and cooled so that it can be sliced."*

> *Example #2:* *"For want of a nail the shoe was lost; for want of a shoe the horse was lost; for want of a horse the knight was lost; for want of a knight the battle was lost; and all for the want of a nail."*

> *Example #3:* *"A great deal of work went into the project, beginning with the initial conception of the toy by our design team. After a lengthy development period, which included extensive testing of the product, the toy was released to critical acclaim nationwide."*

Exercise 2:

This passage is the end of Edgar Allan Poe's "The Tell-Tale Heart." How does Poe provide a build-up from an ostensibly smooth interview with the police to a violent confession? List the words and phrases that indicate the build-up to the climactic ending.

Student answers will vary and may not include every one of the build-ups identified, but most that are underlined should be listed.

> The officers were satisfied. My manner had convinced them. I was <u>singularly at ease</u>. They sat and while <u>I answered cheerily</u>, they <u>chatted</u> of familiar things. But, ere long, I felt myself <u>getting pale and wished them gone</u>. My <u>head ached</u>, and I fancied a <u>ringing in my ears</u>; but still they sat, and still chatted. The <u>ringing became more distinct</u>: I talked more freely to get rid of the feeling: but it continued and <u>gained definitiveness</u>—until, at length, <u>I found that the noise was not within my ears.</u>
>
> No doubt I now grew very pale; but I talked more fluently, and with a <u>heightened voice</u>. Yet the <u>sound increased</u>—and what could I do? It was a low, dull, quick sound—much such a sound as a watch makes when enveloped in cotton. <u>I gasped for breath</u>, and yet the officers heard it not. I talked <u>more quickly, more vehemently</u> but the <u>noise steadily increased</u>. I <u>arose and argued</u> about trifles, in a high key and with <u>violent gesticulations</u>; but the noise steadily increased. Why would they not be gone? <u>I paced the floor</u> to and fro with heavy strides, as if <u>excited to fury</u> by the observations of the men, but the noise steadily increased. O God! what could I do? <u>I foamed—I raved—I swore!</u> <u>I swung the chair</u> upon which I had been sitting, and grated it upon the boards, but the noise arose over all and continually increased. <u>It grew louder—louder—louder!</u> And still the men chatted pleasantly, and smiled. Was it possible they heard not? Almighty God!—no, no? <u>They heard!—they suspected!—they KNEW!</u>—they were making a mockery of my horror!—this I thought, and this I think. But anything was better than this agony! Anything was more tolerable than this derision! I could bear those

hypocritical smiles no longer! I felt that I must scream or die!—
and now—again—**hark! louder! louder! louder! LOUDER!**—

"Villains!" I shrieked, "dissemble no more! I admit the deed!
—tear up the planks! —here, here!—it is the beating of his
hideous heart!

Device #17   ***Parallelism/Chiasmus:***

To communicate is to speak, to pause, and to listen.
To listen, to pause, and then to speak is to communicate well.

Parallelism is one of the most important of organizational devices at a writer's or speaker's disposal. It consists of using the same general structure for multiple parts of a sentence, or for multiple sentences, in order to link them all, as in this famous one from Winston Churchill: *"The inherent vice of capitalism is the unequal sharing of blessing; the inherent virtue of socialism is the equal sharing of miseries."* *Parallelism* gives your writing a sense of overall cohesion, keeping it balanced and intentional throughout.

There is no part of speech or type of sentence that can't be paralleled in some circumstances. By matching the cadence, the form, or the subjects (note the noun/prepositional phrase parallelism in the previous phrasing), you'll be able to make your esay easier to read and digest and your speeches easier to listen to. *Parallelism* is particularly useful for keeping long lists understandable or for making long parenthetical comments less cumbersome (note the parallelism: "useful for keeping...or for making..."). This first sample gives an example of this common usage:

> *Example #1:* *"The manor—designed for beauty and*
> *grace, built for durability and strength,*
> *and located for privacy and safety—was the*
> *ideal home for those three children."*

While parallelism usually matches the syntax of the various elements, this technique isn't always necessary. In the second sample, we see an example of a parallelism that uses differing syntax. Linking the overall feel of each clause, however, still allows the units to seem tied together.

> *Example #2:* *"The burglar shinnied up the drainpipe,*
> *delicately opened the window that had*
> *conveniently been left unlocked, stealthily*
> *forced his body through, and crashed down*
> *loudly on the kitchen floor."*

Feel free to try *parallelism* in different contexts, always asking yourself whether it helps make your writing more readable. A good parallel structure is stylistically pleasing, natural feeling, and structurally supportive.

Chiasmus is a special form of *parallelism* that flips the original form around. While a *parallelism* might be simply, *"He smiled happily and laughed joyfully,"* a *chiasmus* of that same sentence could be, *"He smiled happily and joyfully laughed."* Notice how the *parallelism* is a verb and adverb followed by a parallel verb and adverb, whereas the *chiasmus* is a verb and adverb, followed by an adverb and verb in an inverted order.

Chiasmus is stylistically more ornate than standard *parallelism* and can lend some extra impact to your statement. Some sentences work best in a parallel structure, while others sound better as a *chiasmus*. There is no hard and fast rule about when to use which. When in doubt, you should try them both and think about which sounds more natural.

> *Example #3: "I have journeyed in the lands of the spirit, drunk from the fountains of wisdom, rested beneath the trees of eternity, and, to the land of my birth, I have returned."*

Exercise 1:

The first 5 statements that follow, paraphrases of well-known statements, are not necessarily incorrect, but are much stronger through either *parallelism* or *chiasmus*. Rewrite them and note the difference. The next 5 are not famous statements, but can be improved in the same way. Rewrite each of the statements and then explain why you made the change(s) you did. *The first one has been done for you as an example.*

Answers will vary, but should resemble the following examples.

1. It is completely human to err, but to forgive is divine.
    Revision: *To err is human, to forgive divine.*
    Explanation: *The revision saves words and has the "punch" of using the infinitive as subject of both clauses. Here we have both parallelism and antithesis.*

2. It was not their prerogative to question why they were being ordered to charge; their only option was to charge and be killed.

   Revision: **Theirs was not to question why; theirs was but to do and die.**

   Explanation:

3. Don't ask what your country can do for you. Instead, try thinking about what you can do for your country.

   Revision: **Ask not what your country can do for you. Ask what you can do for your country.**

   Explanation:

4. Dying is like sleeping, but then you have to think about what dreams might come when you fall asleep, and that's the problem.

   Revision: **To die—to sleep. To sleep, perchance to dream; aye there's the rub. For in that sleep of death, what dreams may come must give us pause.**

   Explanation:

5. All of us will defend any one of us, and each of us will sacrifice himself or herself for the group.

   Revision: **All for one and one for all.**

   Explanation:

6. An optimist sees an opportunity in every calamity, while just the opposite is true for a pessimist.

   Revision: **An optimist see an opportunity in every calamity; a pessimist sees a calamity in every opportunity.**

   Explanation:

7. When a nation is strong, it is not always just. And when justice becomes a trait it values, it loses some of its strength.

   Revision: **When a nation is strong, it is not always just. When it strives to be just, it is no longer strong.**

   Explanation:

8. The successful candidate will demonstrate an ability to work under pressure, a willingness to work flexible hours, have at least a bachelor's degree and three years' experience, and sincerely wish to be of service to others.

   Revision: **The successful candidate will demonstrate an ability to work under pressure, a willingness to work flexible hours, and a sincere wish to be of service to others. Only candidates with at least a bachelor's degree and three years' experience will be considered.**

   Explanation:

9. Democracy demands responsibility, but for tyranny to prosper, the people must be obedient.

   Revision: **Democracy demands responsibility, tyranny demands obedience.**

   Explanation:

10. Good writers value parallelism because it creates a logical information flow, as well as enabling the writer to be concise and emphasize key points.

> Revision: **Good writers value *parallelism* because it creates a logical information flow and enables the writer to emphasize key points concisely.**

Explanation:

11. Her writing reveals not only intelligence, but it is also humorous.

> Revision: **Her writing reveals not only intelligence, but humor as well.**

Explanation:

The writer who understands the rules of language, the principles of rhetoric, and the needs of audience is the writer who succeeds.

Parallelism and *chiasmus* are crucial to structural flow and cohesion. Both involve sentence structure, in that they both use similar constructions in a sentence or series of sentences to create a sense of connection. They use slightly different approaches to convey different meanings, to drive a point home, or to make a piece of writing more readable.

While good *parallelism* will likely not be noticeable, as it produces an evenly toned, flowing narrative, if the *parallelism* is off, readers will be jarred and disconcerted, almost as if an alarm bell has sounded. If a piece of writing seems stilted or difficult to read, the writer may not have been using *parallelism* to its best advantage.

> *Example #1:* *"She dropped her pack to the ground, slipped her boots off, tossed her coat onto a nearby chair, and sank to the floor with a sigh."*

*Example #2: "It would seem that this defensive tactic—
although highly graceful and elegant in
form, rapid and effective in style, and safe
and easy to learn—would never catch on in
the martial arts community."*

Chiasmus involves an inversion of the expected. It is a more ornate version of *parallelism* and is often used to reinforce a statement. A *chiasmus* changes the original form of a structure around. This is in contrast to *parallelism*, in which the structure is retained throughout the sentence. For example, someone might *"eat hastily and clean up thoughtlessly"* in a parallel sentence. In a *chiasmus*, the person would *"eat hastily and thoughtlessly clean up."*

If you spot *chiasmus*, it usually means that the writer thinks the statement is worthy of closer attention. Ask yourself why the writer might choose to invert the expected form and look for the point your attention is being drawn to. The form is more recognizable than *parallelism* because of the obvious deviation from normal structure. Sentences which include a *chiasmus* might be used in a *climax* or to support an argument.

*Example #1: "We walked briskly along the seawall to
catch the sunset, and quickly realized that
we were too late."* ("walked briskly" vs.
"quickly realized")

Caution: A danger with *chiasmus*, however, is that some readers might criticize a writer's style for failing to keep elements parallel. For this reason, it is best for all but the most accomplished and skilled writers to use *parallelism* exclusively.

Exercise 2:

Eight of these sentences lack *parallelism*. Analyze those sentences that are not parallel in terms of their overall effectiveness and rewrite them.

1. I enjoy running, writing, reading, and the way I can swim.
    The words running, writing, and reading are single word direct objects. "[T]he way I can swim" is a direct object in a clause and should be changed to "swimming" to make the sentence parallel.

2. During my vacation, I plan to watch movies, play golf, and catch fish.

3. The boys enjoyed operating their paper route and the money they made.
    This sentence lacks *parallelism* ("enjoyed" followed by an object and "the money" followed by a clause), but employs a *zeugma*. It would be the writer's decision whether to maintain the *zeugma* or make the sentence parallel.

4. When she was preparing to write, she would sharpen her pencil, and the paper would be organized.
    The sudden passive voice makes it sound as if sharpening her pencil organized her paper. The sentence should read: *when she was preparing to write, she would sharpen her pencil and organize her paper.*

5. Her daughter got her ready for work by wheeling her into the bathroom, helping her into the shower, and selecting what she was going to wear.
    The series, which is composed of gerunds / objects / prepositional phrases, should conclude with a parallel construction, such as "putting her clothing on the bed."

6. The main problems the landlord had were the late rent, the loud noise, and the neighbor's complaining all the time.
    "Late rent" and "loud noise" are noun phrases, while "neighbors complaining" is a participial phrase and should be changed to "neighbor's complaints."

7. F. Scott Fitzgerald is well known for writing lyrical novels, but he is also known for his wild intoxication.
   Stylistically, "wild intoxication" should be changed into a participle/object phrase to make it parallel to "writing lyrical novels," maybe by substituting, "drinking large amounts."

8. Would you please pick up your room, fold your laundry, and then come into the kitchen?

9. I don't know why she cannot see through his lies, his deceit, and the tricks that he plays.
   "The tricks that he plays" is not parallel to "lies" and "deceit." The sentence should end with "tricks." The phrase is also redundant. "Deceit" and "tricks that he plays" mean essentially the same thing.

10. Their children were known for their honesty, determination, and for playing pranks in the neighborhood.
    Again, "honesty" and "determination" are nouns and "playing pranks..." is a participial phrase. Some alternatives might be: "...telling the truth, trying again and again, and playing pranks..." or "honesty, determination, and mischief..."

Exercise 3:

The following is President Abraham Lincoln's Gettysburg Address. Analyze the President's use of *parallelism* and *chiasmus*; they have been underlined for you. Notice how Lincoln's use of these devices helps to clarify his points and create a sense of eloquence to this very short speech.

Fourscore and seven years ago our fathers brought forth on this continent, a new nation, <u>conceived in Liberty, and dedicated to the proposition</u> that all men are created equal.

Now we are engaged in a great civil war, testing whether <u>that nation, or any nation so conceived and so dedicated,</u> can long endure. We are met on a great battlefield of that war. We have come to dedicate a portion of that field, as a final resting-place for those who here gave their lives that that nation might live. It is altogether fitting and proper that we should do this.

But, in a larger sense, <u>we can not dedicate—we can not consecrate—we can not hallow</u>—this ground. The brave men, living and dead, who struggled here, have consecrated it, far above our poor power to add or detract. The world <u>will little note, nor long remember what we say here, but it can never forget</u> what they did here. <u>It is for us the living, rather, to be dedicated</u> here to the unfinished work which they who fought here have thus far so nobly advanced. <u>It is rather for us to be here dedicated</u> to the great task remaining before us—that from these honored dead we take increased devotion to that cause for which they gave the last full measure of devotion; that we here highly resolve that these dead shall not have died in vain; that this nation, under God, shall have a new birth of freedom; and that government <u>of the people, by the people, for the people,</u> shall not perish from the earth.

Device #18

Anadiplosis/Conduplicatio:

Repeat key words for emphasis, emphasis that will drive home your key point.

Anadiplosis and *conduplicatio* are two forms of repetition that can help add structure to your essays. While repetition is often thought of as a bad technique in papers—and many teachers warn against it—when used properly, it can be an effective organizational device. As it is with any strategy or device, the key to using it is an awareness of what you are doing and why.

While the repetition of a word makes it stand out from the rest of the text, if the repeated word has no real relevance, its use comes across as awkward and bulky. When the word is a key part of the discussion, however, repetition can help focus the reader's attention on it. Rather than seeming overused, the word takes on extra power and force.

Anadiplosis takes the last word of a sentence or phrase and repeats it near the beginning of the next sentence or phrase. Words used this way end up near one another, so their repetition becomes very apparent. Used well, this form can have a beautiful sound and can be an effective way of putting focus on a key word.

> *Example #1: "In education we find the measure of our own ignorance; in ignorance we find the beginning of wisdom."*

Conduplicatio is similar, but takes an important word from anywhere in one sentence or phrase and repeats it at the beginning of the next sentence or phrase. This form is crucial to good organization within an essay. It will help guide your reader from one idea to the next by aiming directly at the key point of your discussion. Some writers tend to lead into every new point with a long string of words introducing the fact that they are going to talk about a new point (note the awkwardness of this sentence). *Conduplicatio* helps you avoid this inadequacy by introducing the point right at the beginning. This will help your reader follow you more easily and will ultimately result in a stronger paper.

Example #2: *"This law destroys the fruits of thirty years of struggle, bringing us back to a less enlightened time. Law should be evolutionary, building up rather than tearing down."*

Example #3: *"Seeing that they hear, do we not ask if they speak? Seeing that they speak, do we not ask if they reason? Seeing that they reason, do we not question whether we are more alike than not?"*

Exercise 1:

Identify each of the following statements as either a form of *anadiplosis* or of *conduplicatio*. Then, create your own *anadiplosis/conduplicatio* that deal with the underlined topic, which may or may not be the term used in the rhetorical device. (You should have 8 sentences total.) *The first one has been done for you as an example.*

Sentences will vary. Although the topics will be repeated, students should be sure to distinguish between the two forms.

1. **Many early religions forbade <u>freedom</u>. Freedom for them was a way of allowing dissent to flourish.** *Anadiplosis*

Anadiplosis: *Only guards and the warden experienced any type of freedom. For prisoners, freedom was only at the end of their sentences.*

Conduplicatio: *Weightlessness gives astronauts the feeling of an escape from the confines of gravity. Escaping from handcuffs, however, was exactly what was on the mind of the prisoner.*

2. **"<u>Drugs</u> don't just destroy their victims; they destroy entire families, schools, and communities."—Elizabeth Dole** *conduplicatio*

Your sentence on drugs:
Anadiplosis:

Conduplicatio:

3. Queeg: "Aboard my ship, excellent <u>performance</u> is standard. Standard performance is sub-standard. Sub-standard performance is not permitted to exist." —Herman Wouk (*The Caine Mutiny)*   ***anadiplosis***

    Your sentence on performance:
    Anadiplosis:

    Conduplicatio:

4. "Fear leads to anger. Anger leads to hate. Hate leads to <u>suffering</u>."—Yoda (*Star Wars)*   ***anadiplosis***

    Your sentence on suffering:
    Anadiplosis:

    Conduplicatio:

5. "This afternoon, in this room, I testified before the Office of Independent Council and the Grand Jury. I answered their <u>questions</u> truthfully, including questions about my private life—questions no American citizen would ever want to answer."—William Jefferson Clinton   ***conduplicatio***

    Your sentence on questions:
    Anadiplosis:

    Conduplicatio:

Repetition is the soul of memory, memory the soul of knowledge.

While both devices help emphasize a certain word, they also can build a hypnotic rhythm through their repetition. This sort of stylized guiding of your reader towards a beat in your writing is an excellent skill to have. Biblical verse makes extensive use of both *anadiplosis* and *conduplicatio* to move towards a crescendo in a sentence.

> **Anadiplosis:** *In the beginning God made the heavens and <u>the earth.</u> <u>The earth</u> was without form and void, and darkness was upon the face of the deep. (Gen. 1:1-2)*

> **Conduplicatio:** *And the woman said to the serpent, "We may eat the fruit of the <u>garden</u>. But of the fruit of the tree which is in the midst of the <u>garden,</u> God has said, 'You shall not eat it...'" (Gen. 3:2)*

These two can also be used stylistically as an emotional appeal, almost as if you are crying out in repetition. In speech, this is a common way we convey our disbelief or shock at something. By mimicking this behavior in your writing, you can bring your reader to a similar feeling. The first example shows this type of emotional style.

> **Example #1:** *"Did you not weep when the bombs rained down? Did you not weep?"*

> **Example #2:** *"There are few things more important than a warm bed; a warm bed and a shower, perhaps."*

> **Example #3:** *"In life we must always keep aware of the constant ebb and flow. Life is a river, not a face of stone."*

Exercise 2:

These 10 statements could be much more powerful if written to include either *anadiplosis or conduplicatio*. Rewrite each and then explain how the rewritten version is rhetorically superior to the original. *The first one has been done for you as an example.*

1. You will know the truth, and it will set you free.–paraphrased from John 8:32

Rewrite: *You will know <u>the truth</u>, and <u>the truth</u> will set you free.*
Explanation: *Both versions mean the same thing, but the second is much more lyrical, and the repetition emphasizes the idea of "truth." "It" in the original could refer to one's knowledge of the truth.*

Rewrites will vary, but should be similar to these examples.

2. On the victim's wristwatch was a single fingerprint, and it places *you* with the body at the time of death.

   Rewrite: **On the victim's wristwatch was a single fingerprint, a fingerprint that puts you with the body at the time of death.**

   Explanation:

3. Once and for all, I'm going to vary my routine, the one that has defined my every waking moment for the past two decades.

   Rewrite: **Once and for all, I'm going to vary my routine, the routine that has defined my every waking moment for the past two decades.**

   Explanation:

4. The question isn't whether we can win, but whether we can play well.

   Rewrite: **The question isn't whether we can win; the question is whether we can play well.**

   Explanation:

5. The world said, disarm, disclose, or face serious consequences...and, therefore, we worked with it...to make sure that Saddam Hussein heard the message.—paraphrased from a comment made by President George W. Bush, March 21, 2006

   Rewrite: **The world said, disarm, disclose, or face serious consequences...and, therefore, we worked with the world...to make sure Saddam Hussein heard the world's message.**

   Explanation:

6. The patriot does not question; he or she acts.

   Rewrite: **The patriot does not question; the patriot acts.**

   Explanation:

7. ...with firmness in the right as God allows us to see it...—paraphrased from Abraham Lincoln's Second Inaugural Address, March 4, 1865

   Rewrite: **...with firmness in the right as God allows us to see the right...**

   Explanation:

8. Fortinbras says that because Hamlet died a hero's death, he should have an appropriate funeral.

    Rewrite: **Fortinbras says that because Hamlet died a hero's death, he should have a hero's funeral.**

    Explanation:

9. Historians will not be viewing the current administration as a comedy or tragedy, but as a farce—of misunderstanding, miscommunication, and mistaken identity.

    Rewrite: **Historians will not view the current administration as a comedy or tragedy, but as a farce—a farce of misunderstanding, miscommunication, and mistaken identity.**

    Explanation:

10. "For I know the plans I have for you," says the Lord, "to prosper—not harm you; to give you a future and hope."—paraphrased from Jeremiah 29:11

    Rewrite: **"For I know the plans I have for you," says the Lord, "plans to prosper you and not to harm you, to give you a future and a hope."**

    Explanation:

11. Still, some viewed the governor as a prophet of hope in a time when cynicism and despair were the fashion.

    Rewrite: **Still, some viewed the governor as a prophet—a prophet of hope in a time when cynicism and despair were the fashion.**

    Explanation:

Exercise 3:

Write 5 original constructions that employ *anadiplosis* and 5 that employ *conduplicatio*. *The first one has been done for you as an example.*

Answers will vary, but they must be valid examples of *anadiplosis* and/or *conduplicatio*.

Anadiplosis:

1. *You think I wish to harm you? You who have been nothing but a friend to me?*

2.

3.

4.

5.

6.

Conduplicatio:

1. *Music is to the soul as air is to the lungs. Without music, the heart is silent, and it is only in music that wordless emotions find a voice.*

2.

3.

4.

5.

6.

Repeat to emphasize, emphasize to clarify, clarify to instruct.

Anadiplosis and *conduplicatio*, when used correctly, keep the intent of a piece of writing clear, and provide transitions between thoughts. Both forms complement a paper well by deliberately repeating a word or key phrase to add importance. If words which do not seem crucial to the argument are repeated, either the writer did not edit with care, or you may be missing the point and should read more closely. For example, the point of the *conduplicatio* certainly is obscure in the following sentence: *"We all enjoyed hearing about Horace's new dog; however, in all that he said, this new dog was not really part of what Horace was so upset about."* Nothing in the first half of the sentence points to Horace's distress in the second half, even though "new dog" is repeated.

Anadiplosis, which repeats the final word of a sentence or phrase in the early part of the following sentence or phrase, also needs to be used with care; it is not in the sentence that follows: *"No one is above the laws of the country that governs; to be governed demands that you be punished."* While it is a correct use of *anadiplosis*, it makes no logical sense and the sentence would be better if it were rephrased without the *anadiplosis*. *Anadiplosis* and *conduplicatio* often appear in persuasive essays to affirm key ideas within the essay. A well-organized essay frequently uses either or both devices so that readers can easily focus on the core concepts of the work.

> *Example #1:* *"It is doubtful that he would have fully recovered without the rapid intervention of hand surgery—surgery that allowed him to regain a full range of motion within months."*

> *Example #2:* *"This type of segregation is not just harmful to our children. Segregation is also harmful to the larger community it is practiced in."*

When you see these techniques being used, ask yourself why the writer felt the need to draw your attention to a particular point. Also, ask yourself if the use supports the essay or detracts from it.

Exercise 4:

The following is a short passage from Father Mapple's sermon in *Moby Dick*. It has been revised to suit the rhetorical nature of this section. Note any uses of *anadiplosis* and/or *conduplicatio* in this paragraph and analyze the effectiveness of each use, in terms of clarity and eloquence.

And now the time of tide has come; the ship casts off her cables; and from the deserted wharf the uncheered ship for Tarshish, all careening, glides to sea. That ship my friends, was the first of recorded smugglers! the contraband was Jonah. But the sea rebels; he will not bear the wicked burden. A dreadful storm comes on, the ship is like to break. But now when the boatswain calls all hands to lighten her, they break with haste. When boxes, bales, and jars are clattering overboard, they break also. When the wind is shrieking, and the men are yelling, and every plank thunders with trampling feet right over Jonah's head; in all this raging tumult, Jonah sleeps his hideous sleep; he does not break.

And now the time of tide has come; <u>the ship (1)</u> casts off her cables; and from the deserted wharf the uncheered <u>ship (2)</u> for Tarshish, all careening, glides to sea. That <u>ship (3),</u> my friends, was the first of recorded smugglers! the contraband was Jonah. But the sea rebels; he will not bear the wicked burden. A dreadful storm comes on, <u>the ship (4)</u> (*CONDUPLICATIO*) is like to <u>break (A)</u>. But now when the boatswain calls all hands to lighten her, they <u>break (B)</u> with haste. When boxes, bales, and jars are clattering overboard, they <u>break (C)</u> also. When the wind is shrieking, and the men are yelling, and every plank thunders with trampling feet right over Jonah's head; in all this raging tumult, Jonah sleeps his hideous sleep; he does not <u>break. (D)</u> (*ANADIPLOSIS*)

Device #19   ***Metabasis:***

Before we continue, let's consider the devices we've already covered and anticipate what is still to come...

Metabasis is a device used to sum up a body of work that has come before, so that you can move on to a new point: *"I have discussed various reasons that show why we need to vote for a new president of this company: our present leader has run the organization for twelve years, she has not had any profitable ideas in years, her salary has doubled since 2005, the company's stock has not moved, and her daughter has recently been hired as a consultant. But last week, the final incident occurred that has led me to recommend that she be replaced."* It is a very important organizational tool in long essays and papers, but its use is limited in shorter papers.

After covering a range of topics, it can be helpful to recap them quickly to help your reader see your overall motive. Sometimes, over the course of a few pages, the thread of an argument or topic can be lost, even in the best written papers. *Metabasis* gives you the chance to tell your readers exactly what you were doing and to remind them of the most crucial areas you covered. After doing that, you are ready to move on to a new section, different from, but related to, the first.

Metabasis usually takes a regular form, something along the lines of, *"I have discussed cars and factories, and how these relate to global warming, but we have still to look at long-term atmospheric trends."* Many writers use *metabasis* to bring up important points that are not directly related to the main thrust of the earlier sections, while others use it to introduce a concluding section. *Metabasis* may also be used as a way to bring up a contrasting opinion or way of looking at something. By first listing the various points you have assembled for one side of the argument, you effectively arrange them neatly and orderly into their own grouping. That leaves you free to begin a new, opposing discussion, with a clear demarcation between the two.

In practice, it is rarely necessary to summarize anything less than four or five pages of material; the average reader is more than capable of keeping that amount clear in his or her head. If used in shorter papers, you run the risk of speaking down to your readers—or worse, of coming across as repetitive in your writing.

Example #1: *"Having dealt as we have with the many devices used by a writer in his craft, we shall now proceed to examine those devices a reader may make use of to analyze a piece of literature."*

Example #2: *"I have laid out for you neatly and in proper array the various flaws in the current system. Let me next offer you workable alternatives."*

Example #3: *"The previous passages explain when they got here, and who brought them. The next quotation shows how and why they made the journey."*

Exercise 1:

Write 5 original constructions that employ *metabasis*. On at least some of them, try to avoid using any form of the first person. *The first one has been done for you as an example.*

Answers will vary, but they must be valid and original examples of *metabasis*.

1. *Up to now, we've focused on* rhetorical *devices that help the writer strategically. Now we will explore those that help him or her organize an essay.*

2.

3.

4.

5.

6.

As we see in the three example sentences that follow, *metabasis* is often integrated into a transitional paragraph or conclusion within the work. <u>*Metabasis*</u> repeats the key points of the previous section for the reader so that the focus of the piece remains clear. A lengthy piece of writing that is well organized may use this device in several places to maintain the overall force of the argument.

This organizational device usually takes the form of a sentence or series of sentences summing up key points. The writer may also introduce new concepts here, with a statement such as, *"Now that we have covered politicians and their agendas, along with their relationship to the news media, it is also important to consider campaign finances."*

Thus, when a writer uses *metabasis*, it is a sign that a transition is in store, or a conclusion is being drawn. It is important to pay attention to the points the writer believes to be most salient or supportive of a final argument. Also, you should consider whether the writer has adequately explained the points fully. Has the writer fully established the point now wrapping up, or is the writer using *metabasis* as a means of closing a discussion that is not yet complete?

This device also alerts you to a potential change in topic or tone that you should be prepared for.

Example #1: *"As we have seen, arguments for an increased minimum wage include higher costs of living and recognition of changes in the way taxes are applied. However, the perspective on minimum wages changes when you are a small business owner, rather than an employee."*

Example #2: *"As stated above, all three of these issues are crucial when one considers the existing public transit system. By implementing the workable changes suggested, the system could be made workable again."*

Example #3: *"Now that we have examined the way in which these ideas are used in Shakespeare's plays, it is important to look at the work of his contemporaries to judge how revolutionary these ideas really were."*

Exercise 2:

The passage excerpt that follows begins to examine two views of autumn. The writer has chosen to use *metabasis* as her transition from one view to the opposite. Read the passage and evaluate the use of *metabasis*. Does her use of the device help the piece or detract from its effectiveness?

Answers will vary, but students must take into consideration the complexity of the points that are transitioned and the overall length of the text to determine whether the *metabasis* is effective or even necessary.

The third season of the year is autumn, and it delivers many lovely gifts as the earth passes the prime of its year. The period that transitions the world from summer to winter is the time when deciduous trees retreat into themselves. As we look at trees and shrubs shedding their leaves and fruit, we tend to think of death. But this is not death, it is the first stage of rejuvenation. Thus, autumn is the beginning of spring.

This beginning of spring is a showcase of beauty in its own right. As the days grow cooler and the number of daylight hours decreases, deciduous trees and shrubs slowly lose the chlorophyll that gives the leaves their green color. With the fading of the green, emerge the gorgeous yellows and flaming reds. Finally, the leaves fall from their branches, and we know that the preparation for rebirth has begun. The leaves return to the earth to become nourishment for future generations.

Trees, however, are not the only living things for which autumn is the beginning of renewal and not the end of life. In fact, all of nature's flora is becoming pregnant. In about six months, new "babies" will be born of every living tree, plant, flower, and shrub. We can witness how the earth takes back from its green life everything that was on loan during the growing season.

This glorious hour of nature is to be admired and enjoyed. It is a privilege to see life in the making and to watch the land go to sleep for its long rest. Autumn is the most optimistic of seasons, acknowledging that the arrival of winter is indeed a certainty, but knowing also that the arrival of another spring is just as certain.

<u>Having explored the positive view of the year's final months, it is probably also appropriate to acknowledge that another, far different, view is also possible.</u> Some believe that the season of the year that arrives just in time to ruin the summer is named as a description for what they do mentally and emotionally after the beautiful summer sun retreats to below the equator. Such people believe that there is nothing good about fall except football...

Exercise 3:

Here is a revised version of Lincoln's Gettysburg Address that uses *metabasis* as the primary transition between the varying views. Read the passage and evaluate these uses of *metabasis*, which are underlined.

Here, in all three cases, the *metabasis* is clearly ineffective. In fact, it destroys the simple eloquence and flow of the speech.

Fourscore and seven years ago our fathers brought forth on this continent, a new nation, conceived in Liberty, and dedicated to the proposition that all men are created equal.

<u>Now, having explored the principle on which this country was founded, let us pause to lament our current situation.</u> Now we are engaged in a great civil war, testing whether that nation, or any nation so conceived and so dedicated, can long endure. We are met on a great battlefield of that war. We have come to dedicate a portion of that field, as a final resting-place for those who here gave their lives that that nation might live. It is altogether fitting and proper that we should do this.

<u>Realizing, then, our purpose, and agreeing that it is a right and proper purpose, we must examine whether it is, indeed, an achievable purpose.</u> But, in a larger sense, we can not dedicate—we can not consecrate—we can not hallow—this ground. <u>Those actions would seem premature and insufficient; therefore what should be our next step?</u>

The brave men, living and dead, who struggled here, have consecrated it, far above our poor power to add or detract.

The world will little note, nor long remember what we say here, but it can never forget what they did here. It is for us the living, rather, to be dedicated here to the unfinished work which they who fought here have thus far so nobly advanced. It is rather for us to be here dedicated to the great task remaining before us—that from these honored dead we take increased devotion to that cause for which they gave the last full measure of devotion; that we here highly resolve that these dead shall not have died in vain; that this nation, under God, shall have a new birth of freedom; and that government of the people, by the people, for the people, shall not perish from the earth.

Device #20 **Parenthesis:**

***Here is where you will learn how to handle supplemental material,
material that helps to expand and clarify your ideas.***

Parenthesis is a device that is used to insert an aside or additional information into the main flow of your writing. One way to do this is by using the actual *parenthesis* symbols, although using dashes or commas is also common. Many writing teachers instruct their students to avoid the use of parentheses (the punctuation marks), believing that the actual marks ( ) lessen the effect of whatever is inside them. Note that the previous sentence contains two instances of the device. A number of style guides reiterate this, with some going so far as to say that anything put within parentheses probably isn't important enough to be included in a finished product!

The use of commas and dashes to set off parenthetical material helps you say the crucial things you have to say, without having to end your sentence first. It is an organizational godsend, the written equivalent of the spoken "aside."

For formal, academic writing, commas are most commonly used to set off parenthetical material. Dashes should be used only when you really want to jolt your readers and make them pay attention to what you have to say. Dashes completely break the written flow, and they are best used when introducing surprising facts or viewpoints, contradictory information, or interruptions. Dashes also lend a less formal, slightly conversational tone to your writing. Commas are a calmer version of dashes, but since there are so many other sentence elements set apart by commas, a long sentence might become confusing.

In addition to focusing a bit more of the spotlight on whatever point you wish to make, parenthetical expressions can also be used to place a bit of information into a context to help your reader better understand your point.

Example #1: *"This continued for many years—some would say far longer than it should have—before a new brand of politician put an end to it."*

Example #2: *"On Christmas Day, 1492, the ship, 70 feet long, with three masts and a crew of 28 men, ran aground on the coast of Haiti."*

*Example #3: "The governor—fool that he is—vetoed the
bill even after it passed both houses of the legislature
unanimously."*

Exercise 1:

Over the next week or so, pay attention to the newspapers, magazines, or
blogs that you read. Listen closely to people you hear speaking, whether
on television, radio, online, or in person. Note any examples of *parenthesis*
usage (the insertion of parenthetical material, not exclusively the use
of parentheses) you encounter and list them. Also, decide whether each
particular construction was effective or not and explain why. *The first one
has been done for you as an example.*

**Answers will vary, but they must be valid examples of
parenthesis, and students must cite their sources, evaluate their
effectiveness, and explain the meaning that is carried by the use
of the device.**

1. Parenthesis: *Scientists in Peru have been sent to collect samples of an
   unidentified object, believed to be a meteorite, which fell...*

   Source: *ABC News online*

   Effective or not: *effective*

   Explanation: *The parenthetical "believed to be a meteorite" adds
   important information. The object is <u>unidentified</u>, but they
   <u>think</u> it is a meteor.*

2. Parenthesis:

   Source:

   Effective or not:

   Explanation:

3. Parenthesis:

   Source:

   Effective or not:

   Explanation:

4. Parenthesis:
    Source:
    Effective or not:
    Explanation:

5. Parenthesis:
    Source:
    Effective or not:
    Explanation:

6. Parenthesis:
    Source:
    Effective or not:
    Explanation:

7. Parenthesis:
    Source:
    Effective or not:
    Explanation:

Exercise 2:

Now, write 9 original constructions that employ the use of *parenthesis*. Make sure you use commas, dashes, and even parentheses marks. *The first one has been done for you as an example.*

Answers will vary, but they must be valid and original examples of *parenthesis*.

1. *Because it was my birthday, my mother served filet mignon—a delicacy usually reserved for company.*

2.

3.

4.

5.

6.

7.

8.

9.

10.

The use of an aside—especially one that asks the reader to pause on an idea—can be very powerful.

Although many writers shy away from it, *parenthesis* is a valuable tool when used well. It involves inserting a thought or comment as an aside into a piece of writing, either by using parentheses, commas, or dashes. The following example sentence contains two uses of *parenthesis*: *"The Constitution—one of the most important documents in all of recorded history—is admired for its beginning words ('We the People...') because it shows that the power comes from the citizens."* Again, note the difference between the two parenthetical remarks: The first states a nearly universal opinion and is unrelated to the main concept of the sentence. The second is simply an example.

Parenthesis is an excellent way to highlight important points or thoughts because what is inserted parenthetically in a sentence tends to stand out. In addition, *parenthesis* makes a piece feel more accessible, as it often lends itself to expressing the voice of the writer and helps build common ground with the reader.

While parentheses marks can be used to add an aside that further illuminates the material under discussion, they are probably the least effective means of inserting material because many readers have a tendency to skip material contained within parentheses. Commas, however, almost mask the fact that supplemental information is being inserted, and sometimes readers can be duped into accepting information they might question if it were presented less subtly. For example, *"The owners found themselves faced with a strike, much like in 1919, when they threatened to halve the workforce through layoffs,"* or *"Diet and exercise, which are far preferable to surgical weight-loss techniques, require a great deal of discipline and commitment."*

Dashes are used to grab the attention of the reader and tend to be used for surprising or novel statements. For example, *"His product—unlike that of the competition—was actually designed to automate the task, rather than simply making it easier,"* or *"She smiled unpleasantly—undoubtedly thinking of my unhappiness—when she informed me that I would not be passing her class."*

When you see *parenthesis* in action, examine the context. Did the parenthetical comments provide additional information or insight? Did it grip your attention and pique your interest in the material, or were you lulled into glossing over information you might otherwise have questioned?

Exercise 3:

Read the following 5 pairs of sentences and explain what value is added to the sentence by the underlined parenthetical element. Be certain to explain the value of the parenthetical material in deeper terms than merely the inclusion of additional information:

Example:

Morgan's relatives, <u>who had come to America on *The Mayflower*</u>, were among the wealthiest in the state.

OR

Among the wealthiest people in the state were Morgan's ancestors.

Explanation: The main idea in the first sentence is that Morgan's relatives had a lot of money. The information about their arrival on *The Mayflower* is less important, but it is interesting, and is, therefore, parenthetical.

1. Time and energy are often in short supply, but they are important when housetraining a puppy.

   OR

   Time and energy, <u>which are often in short supply</u>, are important when housebreaking a puppy.

   Explanation: **The use of *parenthesis* establishes that the supplemental information is indeed supplemental and nonessential. The main idea is that time and energy are important.**

2. The best way to win at a simple game like tic-tac-toe is to start by taking a corner.

   OR

   The best way to win at tic-tac-toe, <u>a simple game,</u> is to start by taking a corner.

   Explanation: **Here again, we do not want the reader to assume that tic-tac-toe's being a simple game is equal in magnitude to how to win.**

3. Colas contain caramel coloring, but clear sodas do not.

    OR

    Colas, <u>unlike clear sodas</u>, contain caramel coloring.

    Explanation: **Either sentence works here. It all depends on the effect the writer wants to create.**

4. Leonardo DiCaprio, <u>star of *Titanic* and *The Aviator*,</u> is very selective about his roles.

    OR

    Leonardo DiCaprio is very selective about his roles.

    Explanation: **The parenthetical material in the first version clarifies the subject for a reader who might not be familiar with these American films or the actor.**

5. The year 1789, <u>often associated with the beginning of the French Revolution</u>, was a year of political stability in the new United States.

    OR

    The year 1789 is often associated with the beginning of the French Revolution, but it was a year of political stability in the new United States.

    Explanation: **Either sentence will work, depending on the effect the writer wishes to achieve. The first focuses on American stability. The second *contrasts* the French turmoil with American stability.**

Exercise 4:

Read the following 5 examples of *parenthesis* and decide which variation is more effective. Then explain why:

1. Loreena McKennitt, a composer and singer of Celtic music, is appearing in Washington, D.C., next week.

    OR

    Loreena McKennitt is a composer and singer of Celtic music. She is appearing in Washington, D.C., next week.

    Which sentence is better?   **FIRST**   SECOND
    Explanation: **Clearly the main idea is her appearance, not her style.**

2. Fifi, a toy poodle, one raised primarily as a lap dog, held three household intruders, who had broken into the Fifth Avenue apartment of Fifi's owners, at bay for five hours until the owners, Wall Street executive Jameson Seamus and his second wife Edith, came home from the theater, where they had been watching a new musical.

    OR

    Fifi, a toy poodle raised as a lap dog, held three household intruders at bay for five hours. The intruders had broken into the Fifth Avenue apartment of Fifi's owners, Wall Street executive Jameson Seamus and his wife Edith. Fifi held the intruders until the Seamuses came home from the theater and were able to call the police.

    Which sentence is better?   FIRST   **SECOND**
    Explanation: **Too many parenthetical expressions set off by too many commas makes the sentence very difficult to follow.**

3. Edgar Allen Poe was, according to the most recent scholarship, *not* an alcoholic and drug addict.

    OR

    Edgar Allen Poe was *not* an alcoholic and drug addict.
    Which sentence is better?   **FIRST**   SECOND

Explanation: **Without the parenthetical material, the second sentence is merely an unsubstantiated assertion.**

4. Aylisha Moseley, accompanied by her partner of many years, Aldous Pierson-Bomcroft, appeared in a gown designed by new-wave fashion mogul Marcus-Marcus. Hers was an off-the-shoulder, red polyester monstrosity with a paisley shawl, which is certain to cement Ms. Moseley's place on all of this season's worst-dressed lists.

OR

Aylisha Moseley appeared in a gown designed by new-wave fashion mogul Marcus-Marcus. The gown—an off-the-shoulder, red polyester monstrosity with a paisley shawl—is certain to cement Ms. Moseley's place on all of this season's worst-dressed lists.

Which sentence is better?   FIRST   **SECOND**
Explanation: **The first tries to cram too much information—some of it not relevant to the issue of the text—into a single sentence.**

5. Mental illness, a physiological condition like diabetes, should not have the stigma attached to it that it currently endures.

OR

Mental illness is a physiological condition like diabetes and should not have the stigma attached to it that it currently endures.

Which sentence is better?   **FIRST**   **SECOND**
Explanation: **Either one works, depending on the author's intent. The first one assumes that mental illness's physiological nature is accepted and moves on to the assertion. The second one establishes that it is a physiological condition first and then makes the assertion.**

Device #21

Apostrophe:

My friend, if you learn to use apostrophe well, you will surely be a beloved writer.

Apostrophe is a rhetorical device in which the writer breaks out of the flow of the writing to directly address a person or personified object. It should not be confused with the punctuation mark of the same name, to which it has no relation.

The *apostrophe* is a forceful, emotional device. The feeling it evokes is that the writer has become so caught up in what he or she is writing that it is no longer possible to respect the bounds of the narrative. Instead, the text must break free and speak directly to something or someone. The *apostrophe* lets the writer demonstrate this fervor in a way that helps reinforce the central point. The Bible uses *apostrophe* frequently: *"O Death, where is thy sting? O grave, where is thy victory?" (1 Corinthians)*

You will likely find the most use for *apostrophe* in informal writing contexts. Creative writing and persuasive essays that lean heavily on emotional strength are ideal places for *apostrophe*. In formal persuasive and informative essays, using *apostrophe* might seem a bit melodramatic and distracting. When you do use it, you will probably be directing your speech directly at the reader, rather than personifying a thing or concept, as in the third example that follows.

Example #1: *"So the sun set over Paris—Paris, my first love, sultry and secretive, beguiling and shy, how I wanted to hold you forever as the sun went down that summer day."*

Example #2: *"So we near our conclusion, and I must ask you, my wise reader, to bear with me for one more small digression."*

Example #3: *"Liberty, O glorious triumph of man, O mighty force that ends all tyranny! Wherever man shakes off his shackles, there you dwell!"*

Exercise 1:

Over the next week or so, pay attention to the newspapers, magazines, or blogs that you read. Listen closely to people you hear speaking, whether on television, radio, online, or in person. Note any uses of *apostrophe* (direct address of a person or thing, not the punctuation mark) you encounter and list them. Also, decide whether each particular construction was effective or not and explain why. *The first one has been done for you as an example.*

Answers will vary, but they must be valid examples of *apostrophe*, and students must cite their sources, evaluate their effectiveness, and explain how use of the device enhances the text.

1. Apostrophe: *Critics, beware! There's a new film maker in town.*
    Source: *Independent film blog*
    Effective or not: *effective*
    Explanation: *The blogger is not addressing any specific critic, but is railing against the group. The direct address is more effective than simply saying, "critics should be aware...."*

2. Apostrophe:
    Source:
    Effective or not:
    Explanation:

3. Apostrophe:
    Source:
    Effective or not:
    Explanation:

4. Apostrophe:
    Source:
    Effective or not:
    Explanation:

5. Apostrophe:
    Source:
    Effective or not:
    Explanation:

Exercise 2:

Improve the following paragraph by adding 2 examples of *apostrophe*; then explain how and why the additions are improvements.

> *"Whoever undertakes to write a biography binds himself to lying, to concealment, to flummery, and even to hiding his own lack of understanding, since biographical material is not to be had, and if it were it could not be used. Truth is not accessible; mankind does not deserve it"*—Sigmund Freud.

Responses should be obvious *apostrophe*s and improvements, i.e., the student in the guise of Freud commenting on the validity or generality of the statement itself, expanding the meaning, or addressing a prospective biographer directly. Explanations should be complete and logical.

It is obvious, astute reader that you are, that using apostrophe can assist in getting your point across.

    Apostrophe, most often found in creative writing and emotionally charged essays, does allow persuasive writers to emphasize a point with a fervor that supports it, such as, *"O, brave new world, that has such people in't..."* When overused, however, it can feel melodramatic or forced. *Apostrophe* is a favorite tool of propagandists and demagogues, and as the previous quotation from *The Tempest* shows, it was also used by Shakespeare. Another example of a pointed and necessary *apostrophe* is John Donne's famous heart-rending assertion: *"Death, be not proud, though some have called thee / Mighty and dreadful."* To speak directly to the idea of death and say that it has no reason to enjoy its reputation requires a powerful device, and *apostrophe* fits perfectly here.

    Apostrophe involves changing the direction of the narrative to address a person or object, as in the following two examples: *"O, pardon me, thou bleeding piece of earth, / That I am meek and gentle with these butchers!"* and *"Obviously, I would not discuss such a topic with ordinary readers, but you seem like the more intelligent sort and well able to handle this complex concept."* In the first example, which is from *Julius Caesar*, Antony speaks to Caesar's dead body, calling it "earth." Shakespeare has used both *apostrophe* and a form of *metaphor* in the sentence. In the second example, the writer is speaking to the readers, flattering them by stating that they have the ability to comprehend the point that is about to be made.

In less formal writing, *apostrophe* must be handled carefully, or the sentences will seem too flowery and overwrought. This example—or something similar to it—may lead the reader to feel that the writer is too wrapped up in ordinary tasks: *"Cleanliness is the greatest virtue of a kitchen. Oh, cleanliness, with your shining counters and glowing dishes, you are denied to me!"*

When you encounter *apostrophe* in formal writing, which is rare, you should carefully consider how it is used, and whether it truly serves the writer's purpose.

Exercise 3:

The following includes a few *apostrophes*, which we have underlined. What is the emotional impact of each *apostrophe*? To whom is Antony speaking?

> ANTONY
> O mighty Caesar! dost thou lie so low?
> Are all thy conquests, glories, triumphs, spoils,
> Shrunk to this little measure? Fare thee well.
> I know not, gentlemen, what you intend,
> Who else must be let blood, who else is rank:
> If I myself, there is no hour so fit
> As Caesar's death hour, nor no instrument
> Of half that worth as those your swords, made rich
> With the most noble blood of all this world.
> I do beseech ye, if you bear me hard,
> Now, whilst your purpled hands do reek and smoke,
> Fulfill your pleasure. Live a thousand years,
> I shall not find myself so apt to die:
> No place will please me so, no mean of death,
> As here by Caesar, and by you cut off,
> The choice and master spirits of this age.

The address to Caesar's corpse is intended to sway listeners on stage and in the audience to Antony's side, to make them believe that Caesar's assassination was unjust. Antony also uses *apostrophe* in addressing the killers. The audience, especially, must believe Antony's accusations and his opinions of Caesar, or the action that follows would not be a true tragedy in the Shakespearean sense.

Exercise 4:

Write 3 passages of your own in which you use *apostrophe*.
Answers will vary, but must be valid and original examples of
apostrophe.

1.

2.

3.

Device #22   *Enumeratio:*

This section will cover two essential ideas:
what enumeratio is, and when it is appropriately used.

Enumeratio refers to the act of supplying a list of details about something. It is used structurally to expand on a central idea, lending force to that idea by enumerating its many different facets. Use of this device tends to come naturally to people in writing, as important issues beg to be expounded upon.

The form can simply be a list of single words related to the central point, as in this first example.

> *Example #1:* "*I went to the mall, the park, the river, the salon, and, finally, home.*"

It can also go into greater detail in a point-by-point analysis, as in the second example.

> *Example #2:* "*There are three main reasons we should pay attention to this: first, the impact on our home town could be substantial; second, as voting citizens, we have a responsibility to keep abreast of changes in the political structure; and third, if no one pays attention to these things, politicians will have carte blanche to do whatever they choose.*"

Enumeratio may also be effectively combined with *hypophora* as an introduction. You can first ask a question whose answer involves numerous details and then proceed to list them. This can be seen in the famous Elizabeth Barrett Browning poem that begins with the *hypophora*, "*How do I love thee?*" and continues through *enumeratio*, "*Let me count the ways.*"

By spending sufficient time outlining its details, you send a clear message to the reader about the importance of your main idea. *Enumeratio* is a good way to lend special force to a concept, while at the same time giving you a functional way to explain it in greater depth.

Example #3: *"There are plenty of great sites to choose from when visiting Washington, D.C. You can go to the National Mall, the Lincoln Memorial, the Jefferson Memorial, the National Gallery, the Smithsonian, the Library of Congress, Ford's Theatre, and the International Spy Museum, to name just a few."*

Exercise 1:

Write 9 original constructions that employ *enumeratio. The first one has been done for you as an example.*
Answers will vary, but they must be plausible and original examples of constructions using *enumeratio*.

1. *This is actually a multi-step process: Think of an example, write it down, turn it in, and get a good grade.*

2.

3.

4.

5.

6.

7.

8.

9.

10.

Your intentional use of rhetorical devices, especially enumeratio, simile, and parenthesis, will mark you as a skillful writer.

Note how it works in this example: *"How can this be? The problem begins with our schools, which do not provide moral models, discipline, or proper education to our children."* An unknown situation is presented in the question, but when *enumeratio* is added, it becomes obvious that the educational system is being attacked.

Because writers use *enumeratio* on ideas they think are important, readers should be attentive to it when it appears. Since a carefully spelled-out list usually indicates what the writer thinks is important, you may want to take notes or explore the details listed to better understand what the writer is trying to communicate. When overused, however, the technique can be a bit numbing because you may feel overpowered by listed objects or ideas. Writers may ask a question that involves a multi-part answer and then enumerate the details in a response designed to show the concept better.

Example #1: *"He started in the produce aisle, moving to the dairy section for cheese, before picking up bread in the bakery aisle, and finally stopping in the liquor section for some wine."*

Example #2: *"The reasons for this are many, but include the rising cost of crude oil, limited access to secure supplies, threats to global shipping traffic, and the tendency of refineries to place a heavy emphasis on certain products."*

Exercise 2:

Create a sentence in which you use *enumeratio* to describe each of the following topics. *The first one has been done for you as an example.*

Answers will vary.

1. *your favorite holiday*

   The reasons Halloween makes me happy are many, but I certainly enjoy seeing children in their costumes and disguises, I love giving candy and treats to little kids, and sometimes I get a thrill from scaring teenagers when they come begging for sweets.

2. things you like to do during summer vacation

3. where you see yourself in the next five to ten years and how you got there

4. the events that led to a well-known war

5. the cycle of rain formation

6. how to set up an email account

Device #23 *Antanagoge:*

The formal names of these devices might be confusing, but certainly their use is extremely important for someone who wants to be a top-notch writer.

Antanagoge is a way of ordering points to downplay negative points so that the reader feels less strongly about them. This is done by placing a negative point next to a positive one. The statement should be phrased in such a way that it becomes apparent that the benefits more than outweigh the costs of the subject you're discussing. Note the way *antanagoge* is used in this example: *"While cutting automobile pollution may cause car makers to lose money in the short run, the benefits of cleaner air and a decrease in deaths by respiratory diseases are definitely worth the risk to businesses."* The writer has cleverly juxtaposed the negative prospect of losing money with the advantages of cleaner air and, most importantly, with a decrease in deaths. To emphasize the point, both negative and positive are restated again at the end of the sentence through the phrase, *definitely worth the risk*. The example contains *two antanagoge*s.

While admitting flaws in your argument is never fun, if handled properly, it can actually improve your ability to persuade. Acknowledging problems offers you credibility with your reader, and by immediately offsetting those problems with positive aspects, you avoid much of the damage that ignoring the problems might lead.

Make sure when you arrange an *antanagoge* that the scales do tip in your favor. The last thing you want to do is to arrange issues so that the arguments against your point outweigh the arguments for it.

Example #1: *"She can be quick to anger, but when you're in need, she'll always be there."*

Example #2: *"The car might cost a bit more than other models when it's new, but it more than pays for itself by not breaking down nearly so often as cheaper ones."*

Example #3: *"I know that in the past it has failed—and on occasion failed miserably—but advances in technology, massive investments from the private sector, and a changed political climate all make the future much, much brighter."*

Exercise 1:

Write 10 original constructions that employ *antanagoge. The first one has been done for you as an example.*

Answers will vary.

1. *Working may be stressful at times, but my job has paid my son's way through college.*

2.

3.

4.

5.

6.

7.

8.

9.

10.

11.

Exercise 2:

For each of the following topics, think of a positive and negative aspect. Then, write an *antanagoge* to discuss the issues you have raised. Be sure the statements are in favor of your argument, whether positive or negative. *The first one has been done for you as an example.*

Answers will vary. It may be helpful for students to think of multiple positive and negative aspects for the topic before writing the *antanagoge*.

1. speed-reading

Positive: get through books in very little time, cram for exams easily, show off your talents, increase understanding, etc.
Negative: miss the flavor of author's style, miss information, it's a trick, not actual knowledge, etc.
Sentence: Even though speed-reading allows you to get through a book quickly, the course is quite expensive. In addition, reading English requires a sense of style, and some subjects, like math, are unsuitable for speed-reading.

2. a prescription drug

Positive: **treat and/or cure a disease, improve quality of life, etc.**
Negative: **multiple side effects (e.g., weight loss, loss of appetite, fatigue, bruising, etc.)**
Sentence:

3. state and federal taxes

Positive: **taxes provide money for roads, schools, and programs that assist needy people, etc.**
Negative: **taxes are often expensive and take away from people's income. Some don't think they're needed, etc.**
Sentence:

4. an infamous historical figure (choose one)

Positive: **any significant political or social contribution**
Negative: **any significant or minor flaw in character, action, opinion, etc.**
Sentence:

5. the Internet

Positive: **instant global communication, provides outlet for research, etc.**
Negative: **allows for dangers such as pedophiles, children are exposed to questionable materials, etc.**
Sentence:

6. pollution

Positive: **researchers are combating global warming, numerous programs have been established to save natural resources (recycling, carpooling, etc.)**
Negative: **global warming, destruction of rainforests and natural habitats, affects health, etc.**
Sentence:

Our repetition of several of these devices might seem tedious at first, but it will help you learn to recognize and use them in the long run.

Writers use *antanagoge* to downplay the importance of negative points by putting them in close proximity to positive points. Look at this example, *"The smell of this unusual tropical fruit can be quite overpowering, but consumers don't mind that and actually enjoy its delicious taste and intriguing texture."* Skillful writers will use this technique to point to flaws in their argument and address the problems immediately, rather than leaving a reader wondering whether the writer actually recognized the flaws. The credibility of an argument tends to increase when writers admit weak points, and many use this device to their advantage. When writers use *antanagoge*, be certain to analyze the admitted weaknesses and the accompanying positive points on your own, rather than accepting the positive as fact.

Some writers may make a mistake, listing benefits which do not outweigh the downsides of the idea being discussed. A bad example of *antanagoge* might be something like this: *"Being unemployed is not as horrible as people think, simply because the person without a job now has plenty of time to analyze his or her life."* When looking at examples of *antanagoge*, look at all sides of the argument laid out in the sentence carefully to determine whether the writer has actually supported the point or undermined it.

Example #1: *"While it might seem that extensive testing is counterproductive, numerous studies have shown that it is an important part of the evaluative process, and the ultimate result will be more satisfying."*

Example #2: *"When I heard it would take three weeks to be delivered, I began to question why I had ordered the product at all. However, the TV was everything that I dreamed of and well worth the wait."*

Exercise 3:

Choose any 3 topics below and write a sentence or two for each that, first, downplays a negative feature and leads into several positive features, then write a second sentence that moves from the positive to the negative. *The first one has been done for you as an example.*

- **professional wrestling**
- **rap music**
- **teenagers**
- **year-round school**
- **educational television**

1. Topic: **buying locally produced food**

   Negative to Positive: *While it may seem difficult to purchase fruits and vegetables that are grown nearby, doing so reduces the costs involved in transportation, increases the flavor, and supports the local community in which you live.*

   Positive to Negative: *Buying locally grown foods may seem more responsible to the community, but doing so does not mean that local growers farm more responsibly than any others elsewhere, and shopping only in your area makes it impossible to obtain certain foods when they are out of season.*

2. Topic:
   Negative to Positive:

   Positive to Negative:

3. Topic:
   Negative to Positive:

   Positive to Negative:

4. Topic:
   Negative to Positive:

   Positive to Negative:

STYLE

Epithet:

You'll certainly devour this section with carnivorous interest.

Epithet is a common stylistic device, although it can be easily overused. It involves attaching a descriptive adjective to a noun to bring a scene to life or evoke a particular idea or emotion, as in the example, *"The clear-eyed pilot safely landed the plane."* A simple *epithet* may use an adjective related to the noun, such as, *"The tall boy towered above his peers,"* but more complex *epithets* may combine unusual adjectives with nouns for a stronger effect; for example, *"The redemptive clouds hovered close to a parched horizon"* shows the unusual adjectives modifying ordinary nouns to make them more open to interpretation.

The *epithet* is one of the most striking stylistic devices in a writer's toolbox. By connecting an unexpected adjective to a noun, the writer brings the subject alive in the reader's mind. *Epithets* can connect an adjective that is actually associated with the noun *(difficult subject),* or they may use an adjective that is appropriate to the noun on a metaphorical level *(abandoned desire). Epithets* can be used in a less literal sense. In a fearful state, one might look upwards towards the "malevolent stars," or, while overwhelmed with joy, one might look at those same "beneficent stars." The use of *metaphor* in this context is sometimes called a **transferred** *epithet*, because the adjective is being transferred from its normal use to another one where it makes figurative, if not literal, sense.

English has a very large selection of adjectives, and *epithet* is a technique that allows you to craft exactly the image you want. When describing a hot day, for example, you could choose from any number of appropriate choices. If the day were humid as well, you might describe it as "murky heat." If you want to describe it as the beginning of spring after a long winter, you might call it "blossoming heat." If it were so hot it made people walk around in a daze you might call it "stupefying heat." The possibilities are as diverse as the English language and as open as your imagination.

Although *epithets* can be beautiful and add a great deal to your writing, there are a couple of things to watch for when using them. Try to stay away from clichéd adjective-noun combinations whenever possible. Phrases like "joyful laughter" or "stunning view" have been seen so often that your reader is unlikely to get any real enjoyment out of them. Part of the beauty of an *epithet* is the ability to surprise and entertain your reader, and falling back on clichés makes that impossible. You also want to avoid overusing *epithets*, especially to describe the same thing. The *epithet* can be an early introduction to an idea, used to make it seem exciting, and followed by more common descriptions of that idea. It can also serve as a crowning presentation of an idea, coming after a number of normal descriptions of the same idea to lay the groundwork.

> *Example #1:* "*On the day of the historic battle, the*
> *ferocious sun rose early and looked bloody.*"

> *Example #2:* "*A healing wind blew through the diseased*
> *hospital.*"

> *Example #3:* "*It's a mesmerizing argument, but if you*
> *keep your focus you'll see it for what it*
> *really is.*"

Epithets, however, need to make sense when they are examined; otherwise they are useless, as in this example: *"I wandered into the negative desert with nothing on my feet except a pair of muscular sandals."* While the *epithets* sound plausible, if you look closely at "negative desert" and "muscular sandals," neither one are logical uses of the device; they are in the sentence simply to be there, not to add to the reader's understanding, nor to the description.

Exercise 1:

Write 10 original constructions that employ *epithet*. *The first one has been done for you as an example.*

Answers will vary, but they must be plausible and original *epithets*. Students should avoid those *epithets* that are written simply for effect and are not suitable.

1. *The farmers anxiously scanned the mocking sky for any sign of rain.*

2.

3.

4.

5.

6.

7.

8.

9.

10.

11.

Exercise 2:

Create an original sentence that uses each of the following nouns in an *epithet*. Then, describe what effect the *epithet* has on the sentence. *The first one has been done for you as an example.*

Answers will vary. Students should be able to explain the logic and intended impact of their choices.

1. Word: smile

   Sentence: *The millionaire's new bride said, "I do," with a ravenous smile.*

   Effect: *Describing the smile as ravenous strongly suggests the bride's greedy motive.*

2. Word: hope

   Sentence:

   Effect:

3. Word: sunrise

   Sentence:

   Effect:

4. Word: jealousy

   Sentence:

   Effect:

5. Word: voice
    Sentence:

    Effect:

6. Word: field
    Sentence:

    Effect:
7. Word: mango
    Sentence:

    Effect:

8. Word: goddess (Greek Or Roman)
    Sentence:

    Effect:

9. Word: painting
    Sentence:

    Effect:

10. Word: soldier
    Sentence:

    Effect:

As a reader, you'll be refreshed by the writer's mouthwatering use of this device.

You may notice as you read a piece of writing that it seems jaded or dull. This can be due to the poor use of *epithets*. For example, most readers are abundantly familiar with terms like "raging fire," "angry tears," or "winsome maidens." Some writers tend to overuse *epithets*; these writers amplify every noun and exhaust the reader by the end of the piece.

A well-constructed *epithet* involves an unusual and distinctive use of an adjective to further qualify a noun. Writers often use *epithets* in essays as part of an introduction or *climax* to lend particular weight to an idea. An *epithet* should surprise and delight you with an interesting use of language that makes a scene or concept more vivid, without seeming ridiculous, overblown, or clichéd.

> *Example #1:* *"Glossy hair rippled over powerful muscles as the horses ran free in the pasture."*
>
> *Example #2:* *"An amazing tree rose before us, easily over three hundred feet tall and covered in small, silvery leaves."*
>
> *Example #3:* *"The verdict changed the hostile atmosphere into one of celebration."*

Exercise 3:

Below are three famous soliloquies in which Shakespeare displays his skillful use of *epithets*. Read the scenes and identify each *epithet*. Then choose 7 and describe the impact each rhetorical use has on the passage.

Answers will vary, depending on the source and the *epithets* selected.

Example:

Epithet: "the slings and arrows of outrageous fortune"

Source: *Hamlet*

Intent: The idea is to make the reader see that Hamlet feels that fate (*fortune*) can be merciless, unpredictable, and dangerous.

Impact: The *epithet* allows the reader to better understand Hamlet's reasoning and outlook about life.

from *Henry IV, Part 1,* Act I, scene ii:

PRINCE HAL:

I know you all, and will awhile uphold
The unyoked humor of your idleness:
Yet herein will I imitate the sun,
Who doth permit the **base contagious clouds**
To smother up his beauty from the world,
That, when he please again to be himself,
Being wanted, he may be more wonder'd at,
By breaking through the **foul and ugly mists**
Of vapours that did seem to strangle him.
If all the year were playing holidays,
To sport would be as tedious as to work;
But when they seldom come, they wish'd for come,
And nothing pleaseth but **rare accidents.**
So, when this **loose behavior** I throw off
And pay the debt I never promised,
By how much better than my word I am,
By so much shall I falsify men's hopes;
And like **bright metal** on a **sullen ground,**
My reformation, glittering o'er my fault,
Shall show more goodly and attract more eyes
Than that which hath no foil to set it off.
I'll so offend, to make offence a skill;
Redeeming time when men think least I will.

from *Hamlet,* Act III, scene iii:

CLAUDIUS:

O, my offence is rank it smells to heaven;
It hath the **primal eldest curse** upon't,
A brother's murder. Pray can I not,
Though inclination be as sharp as will:
My stronger guilt defeats my strong intent;
And, like a man to double business bound,
I stand in pause where I shall first begin,
And both neglect. What if this **cursed hand**
Were thicker than itself with brother's blood,
Is there not rain enough in the **sweet heavens**
To wash it white as snow? Whereto serves mercy
But to confront the visage of offence?
And what's in prayer but this two-fold force,
To be forestalled ere we come to fall,
Or pardon'd being down? Then I'll look up;
My fault is past. But, O, what form of prayer
Can serve my turn? 'Forgive me my **foul murder**'?
That cannot be; since I am still possess'd
Of those effects for which I did the murder,
My crown, mine own ambition and my queen.
May one be pardon'd and retain the offence?
In the **corrupted currents** of this world
Offence's **gilded hand** may shove by justice,
And oft 'tis seen the **wicked prize** itself
Buys out the law: but 'tis not so above;

from *All's Well That Ends Well,* Act I, scene i:

HELENA:

O, were that all! I think not on my father;
And these great tears grace his remembrance more
Than those I shed for him. What was he like?
I have forgot him: my imagination
Carries no favor in't but Bertram's.
I am undone: there is no living, none,
If Bertram be away. 'Twere all one
That I should love a bright particular star
And think to wed it, he is so above me.
In his **bright radiance** and **collateral light**
Must I be comforted, not in his sphere.
The ambition in my love thus plagues itself:
The hind that would be mated by the lion
Must die for love. 'Twas pretty, though plague,
To see him every hour; to sit and draw

His <u>arched brows</u>, his <u>hawking eye</u>, his curls,
In our heart's table—heart too capable
Of every line and trick of his <u>sweet favor</u>.
But now he's gone, and my <u>idolatrous fancy</u>
Must sanctify his relics.

1. Epithet:

    Impact:

2. Epithet:

    Impact:

3. Epithet:

    Impact:

4. Epithet:

    Impact:

5. Epithet:

    Impact:

6. Epithet:

    Impact:

7. Epithet:

    Impact:

Device #25

Asyndeton/Polysyndeton:

Asyndeton is one of the best, most expressive, effective rhetorical devices there is, while polysyndeton is interesting and instructional and stylish.

Asyndeton and *polysyndeton* are two forms that add stylistic force to your writing by handling conjunctions in non-standard ways. *Asyndeton* leaves out conjunctions in a list or between clauses *("He was tall, dark, handsome"),* while *polysyndeton* puts a conjunction between every item *("We have an army and soldiers and tanks and planes.").*

Asyndeton can be used for a number of different reasons. When there are only two items, such as, *"It was a great prize, a reward for years of service,"* *asyndeton* defines the second item as a clarification of the first. It can give the impression that the list you have created was spontaneous, rather than being thought out beforehand and structured in a traditional way. It also may suggest that the list isn't quite finished, and thus leaves your readers to come up with additional items on their own. Most importantly, it gives the feeling of fast movement to your writing, rather than a list that drags out. For example, *"They sat under one roof, princes, dukes, barons, earls, kings."*

Polysyndeton is the stylistic opposite of *asyndeton*, although its effect is not necessarily the reverse. The general feel of *polysyndeton* is one of an increasing urgency and power, with an almost hypnotic rhythm forming quite quickly *("The runner passed the ten-mile mark and the fifteen and the twenty, and the finish line loomed in front of him.").* Polysyndeton is very widely used in the Bible and other religious texts, and its use often brings to mind a comparison to scripture. The conjunctions being used in *polysyndeton* become punctuated beats making a steady cadence that carries on throughout the list, but the punctuation itself is usually determined by the writer, as you can see by looking at the commas and lack of commas in all the examples: *"We listen to hear screams, and cries, and howls of rage."* *Polysyndeton* is also a sure way to give an important list of attributes or ideas immediate force. For example, *"The banquet table was a riot of beef and pork and lamb and fish and fresh vegetables and candied fruits and all sorts of wonderful dainties."*

Both *asyndeton* and *polysyndeton* are powerful rhetorical devices when used sparingly. If you overuse either one, it will quickly lose its power and may even come across simply as grammatical mistakes on your part. Save these devices for the moments when they can best make a list jump off the page or resonate with extra power or pull your reader even further under your spell.

Exercise 1:

Make a list of objects in your bedroom, classroom, or any place else that is very familiar to you. Imagine two different people describing this space from two different points of view. Write two different descriptions of this space. In one, use *asyndeton*; in the other, use *polysyndeton*. Explain your purpose and intended effect in each instance.

Answers will vary, but one of the descriptions must employ *asyndeton*, and the other must use *polysyndeton*.

Asyndeton and *polysyndeton* both add a particular tone to a written work by using conjunctions in non-traditional ways. For example, they are used to build lists, either to make them easier to read or more impressive, or to catch the reader up in a hypnotic beat. *Asyndeton*, leaving conjunctions out entirely, is often used to provide a sense of casual familiarity or to make a list less monotonous to read. It also implies rapid movement, bringing you briskly through the material to arrive at a *climax*, conclusion, or the next section of the writing. *Asyndeton* often appears when a writer wants a sentence to appear less structured or contrived, or to imply that you could continue the list with your own ideas.

> *Example #1:* "*Jockeying for room on the table were turkey, gravy, mashed potatoes, pies, rolls, butter, cranberry sauce, a cornucopia of vegetables.*"

> *Example #2:* "*First-century Jerusalem was a truly multilingual city with Greek, Latin, Aramaic, Hebrew all competing to be heard in a veritable Tower of Babel.*"

Polysyndeton, inserting a conjunction between every item or clause, is often used to build to a *climax* or to provide a list with a sense of impressive power. This technique is often used in Biblical writing to give text added force. *Polysyndeton* is recognizable because it takes a very distinctive form, and therefore a skilled writer will use it infrequently. When a writer presents items using *polysyndeton,* your attention will be drawn more to each individual item than to the list as a whole.

Example #3: "His hair and face and eyes and mouth combined to form an image of absolute power." Note that the lack of commas gives this example a complete picture of the face.

Example #4: "I slithered under the sheets, and under the blankets, and under the top quilt to evade the monsters." Note that here, the commas draw out the action and make escaping more suspenseful.

Exercise 2:

Over the next week or so, pay attention to the newspapers, magazines, or blogs that you read. Listen closely to people you hear speaking, whether on television, radio, online, or in person. Note any uses of *asyndeton* and *polysyndeton* you encounter and list them. Also decide what you think the person's intent was in using this device and evaluate the intellectual, psychological, or emotional impact these devices had on you.

Answers will vary, but they must be valid examples of *asyndeton* and/or *polysyndeton*, and the student must cite the source of the device and evaluate how it functions, considering both its intended impact and its actual impact.

1. Asyndeton:
   Source:
   Intent:

   Impact:

2. Asyndeton:
   Source:
   Intent:

   Impact:

3. Asyndeton:
   Source:
   Intent:

   Impact:

4. Asyndeton:
   Source:
   Intent:

   Impact:

5. Asyndeton:
    Source:
    Intent:

    Impact:

1. Polysyndeton:
    Source:
    Intent:

    Impact:

2. Polysyndeton:
    Source:
    Intent:

    Impact:

3. Polysyndeton:
    Source:
    Intent:

    Impact:

4. Polysyndeton:
    Source:
    Intent:

    Impact:

5. Polysyndeton:
    Source:
    Intent:

    Impact:

Device #26   ***Zeugma:***

With mastery of this device, join two words and the ranks of skillful writers.

Zeugma is a device in which unexpected items in a sentence are linked together by a shared word. If that sounds rather broad, it is. *Zeugma* can encompass subjects linked together by a verb, pronouns by nouns, direct objects by verbs, adjectival phrases by verbs, etc. Although *zeugma* can be used in a number of different ways, the most common and useful stylistic method is to eliminate the repetition of a verb. For example, rather than saying,

> *"The runner lost the race. The school then canceled his scholarship."*

you could simply say,

> *"The runner lost the race and his scholarship."*

In this basic use, the main verb is understood to hold true for each of the direct objects.

To add a bit more stylistic flair, the same verb can be implied for two objects, but with a different meaning in each usage. Take, for example, the sentence,

> *"The man ran a hundred miles, but out of time."*

In this sentence the verb "ran" is being used in a literal sense at first, with the man literally running a hundred miles, and, then, in an idiomatic sense, it indicates him running out of time.

Another stylistic use of *zeugma* is to postpone introducing the verb until the end, or near the end, of the sentence. Sometimes, in a discussion of syntax, this is called a *periodic sentence* because the most important idea or word is closest to the end of the sentence. This can build a sense of suspense for your reader and elevate the importance of the verb in the sentence. Look at the following:

> *"The teenage sweethearts, the elderly couple, and the flickering candles all danced late into the night."*

Zeugma is a great way to forge strong connections between different parts of your sentence. By making them share the same word to find their meaning, you make the reader see them as very closely related. This sense of interconnectedness is important in making a paper feel cohesive overall, as well as simply being pleasing to read. Many people use *zeugma* without knowing exactly what they're doing, and they later find those sentences to be the most delightful. By learning to intentionally create strong *zeugma*, you are at a great advantage.

Exercise 1:

Write 10 original *zeugmas*. Remember that *any* linking of words, phrases, or clauses with a single word are examples of *zeugma*, but the most stylistically pleasing *zeugmas* involve linking unexpected elements in surprising ways. *The first one has been done for you as an example.*

Answers will vary, but they must be accurate and original zeugmas.

1. *The taste of the food and her decorations pleased me.*

2.

3.

4.

5.

6.

7.

8.

9.

10.

11.

Exercise 2:

Read the following sentences and decide how they could be condensed by using *zeugma*. Rewrite the sentences using this rhetorical device and remove any unnecessary information. *The first one has been done for you as an example.*

Answers will vary. An example for each has been provided.

1. Please discontinue using this machine if you feel pain, if you feel faint or if you become dizzy.
    Discontinue use if you feel pain, faintness or dizziness.

2. The magician, who was also a kleptomaniac, stole the show, and afterwards, he took my wallet.
    The kleptomaniac magician stole the show and then my wallet.

3. After holding the elevator door open, he held my hand during the descent.
    He held the elevator door and my hand.

4. The farmers in the valley grew watermelons and harvested corn, but they became restless.
    The farmers in the valley grew watermelons, corn, and bored.

5. My mother lost her keys and then she lost her coat; she finally lost her temper.
    She lost her keys, her coat, and her temper.

6. The sun rose at dawn and his temperature was higher as well.
    The sun and his temperature rose at dawn.

This section will strive to teach the device and the student.

Zeugma is the technique of linking a number of things in a sentence together by using a shared word, as in, *"The Gypsy read the tea leaves and my mind."* It is often used to draw a sense of interconnectedness between objects because the reader will associate them with each other thanks to the common link. *Zeugma* can also be used to reduce a sense of repetitiveness that may arise from poorly organized sentences.

As you read, look for examples of *zeugma* to see how writers keep their audience in suspense and maintain interest in a topic. *Zeugma*, used in highly stylized ways, by adding a verb at or near the end of a sentence, causes the reader to wonder what all the objects in a sentence are doing: *"Not rain or hail or snow or lack of lights, nothing will stop the game from being played."*

When used deliberately, *zeugma* can be highly effective and elegant. In other cases, the device may seem forced or trite, causing you to miss the point of the sentence entirely.

> *Example #1:* *"On the same day, the judge tried the high-profile murder case and his wife's homemade soup."*
>
> *Example #2:* *"The abandoned dance hall was full of broken glass and hearts."*
>
> *Example #3:* *"I've spent too much time and money on this project and your happiness already."*

Exercise 3:

Rewrite each of the following pairs of sentences into single sentences that contain *zeugmas*. *The first one has been done for you as an example.*

Answers will vary, but they must all be correct usages of *zeugma*. Possible sentence completions are shown.

1. The family had a great deal of money. They did not know what they were going to do with it.

   The family had a great deal of money and no idea what to do with it.

2. I enjoy poetry. I think you are very attractive as well.

    I enjoy poetry and your good looks.

3. Mr. Martini left his job. In his will, he bequeathed three thousand dollars to the poor.

    Mr. Martini left his job and three thousand dollars to the poor.

4. The rainsoaked swimmers spent the day at the mall. While they were there, they spent all of their money.

    The rainsoaked swimmers spent the day and all of their money at the mall.

5. I woke up in the middle of the night. I was having a good dream, too.

    I woke up in the middle of the night and a good dream.

6. Roberto won the race. His victory caused Eustacia to fall in love with him.

    Roberto won the race and Eustacia's heart.

7. The car broke down in the worst part of town. Fear caused the driver to begin crying loudly.

    The car and the driver broke down in the worst part of town.

8. With a stroke of the pen, the teacher lowered Alonzo's grade. This would make it more difficult for Alonzo to pass.

    With a stroke of the pen, the teacher lowered Alonzo's grade and his chances of passing.

9. The custodian hurt his back. This happened when he threw the box of junk in the garbage.

    The custodian threw out the box of junk and his back.

10. Jim and Donna were assigned to cook together on the camping trip. While they cooked together, they became friends.

    Jim and Donna made dinner and friends on the camping trip.

Device #27 **Synecdoche/Metonymy:**

Give an ear to these two handy stylistic devices.

Synecdoche and *metonymy* are two very closely related devices. They deal with using a part of something, or something closely related, to refer to a larger whole. There are a number of generally accepted forms of *synecdoche* and *metonymy,* which readers will easily recognize:

> *Example #1:* "The rancher boasted about how many head of cattle he owned." [synecdoche]

> *Example #2:* "The captain shouted, 'All hands on deck.'" [synecdoche]

> *Example #3:* "The White House answered its critics." [metonymy]

> *Example #4:* "The pen is mightier than the sword." [metonymy]

Synecdoche is the use of a part of something to represent the whole. As in the first two examples, the rancher certainly owned the whole cow, not just the head, and the captain wanted the entire crewmember on deck, not just the hands.

Metonymy allows you to refer to something closely related to the actual object, and use that as a way of referring to the object itself. For example, many people talk about the ruler of a monarchy simply as "the crown," even though the monarch is a person who wears the crown. In the last two examples, the White House cannot speak, so it must have been someone from the President's administration, and a sword could easily break a pen, so the idea must be that the concepts expressed in writing can defeat the might of armies.

These are both very versatile forms, and they have a lot of stylistic flair. You are basically assuming your reader will recognize whatever term you use as code or symbol for a different term, such as *"The thief disguised himself to hide from the law."* You could certainly use "police" for "law," but that would not be an instance of *metonymy.* These two devices can give you a wide range of words to choose from and many ways to express the same thing. The trick, of course, is to make sure that there is no confusion about what you're trying to say, as in this awkward, confusing use of *synecdoche*:

"Terrance's parents bought him new wheels." Without any context, we don't know whether it means a new car, wheels for a bicycle, artificial legs, or potter's tools. The intent is not obvious. Avoid these devices if there is doubt as to what they might mean in a sentence.

One good strategy when using *synecdoche* or *metonymy* is to run them by other people to make sure they know what you're talking about. In the context of an assessment essay, however, this isn't possible, so you will want to stick with more obvious uses that you're sure your reader will understand.

We might also refer to a person by the uniform he or she wears, such as when talking about a military officer presiding over a meeting: *"We could not begin until the brass called us to order."* The line between *metonymy* and *synecdoche* is blurry at best, and it is probably easiest to simply think of them as different versions of the same form.

Synecdoche and *metonymy* can be used in almost any context. As with all stylistic devices, they allow you to surprise and delight your readers and invite them to consider a familiar idea from a new angle. By carefully selecting the part you are going to use to represent the whole (or the object with which to associate the idea), you can also subtly pass judgment on and evaluate the idea you are discussing. For example, in the theater, people are often referred to by their function, often devaluing others who have different functions. Often "the talent" will dismiss "the money's" opinions as having no artistic value at all. Doctors, too, have a tendency to speak of their patients in terms of their disease or malady, and, as a result, physicians have been accused of dehumanizing their patients: *"I'll talk to the black eye in bed 3 as soon as I discharge the nosebleed in bed 7."* Because they can be filled with emotional value and might confuse your reader more than clarify your point, you should save these forms for when especially striking examples come to mind, and when you can use them to not only sound good, but also to drive home your point.

> *Example #1:* *"It is becoming less and less acceptable for a business not to take plastic; gone are the days of cash only."*

> *Example #2:* *"No eye could stay dry when faced with such a truth."*

> *Example #3:* *"The press reported favorably on the event."*

Exercise 1:

Write 10 original statements using *synecdoche* and/or *metonymy*. Remember that these devices help you assign a particular value or quality to what you are discussing, as well as surprise your reader into seeing a familiar idea in a new and interesting way. *The first one has been done for you as an example.*

Answers will vary, but they must be valid and original examples of *synecdoche* and/or *metonymy.*

1. *I once sang in a 200-voice chorus.*

2.

3.

4.

5.

6.

7.

8.

9.

10.

11.

Synecdoche uses part of a concept to refer to the entire idea. For example, a character might say, *"I am going up to bed now,"* meaning that he or she intends to go to sleep. A character might also say, *"The Tigers took home the trophy,"* implying that the team called the "Tigers" won a tournament.

> *Example #1:* *"When the beautician opened her own shop, she took twenty heads with her from the shop where she used to work."*
>
> *Example #2:* *"The Heart Association's fundraiser dinner cost $35 a seat."*
>
> *Example #3:* *"I was amazed at how many mouths they had to feed on such a small income."*

Metonymy refers to things that are so closely related to something that they can serve as a symbol for it. For example, the President of the United States is associated with the Oval Office, and a statement might be said to "come from the Oval Office." Obviously, an office cannot issue a statement, but the elected official who occupies it can.

> *Example #4:* *"The brass showed up unexpectedly and performed a surprise inspection."*
>
> *Example #5:* *"The Throne has issued an order that the troops will be paid by Thursday."*

Exercise 2:

Rewrite the first 5 sentences so they are good examples of *synecdoche* and the last 5 as good examples of *metonymy*. Make sure that the use is clear and obvious. *The first one has been done for you as an example.*

Answers will vary. Suggestions are supplied.

Synecdoche:

1. Boredom—having nothing to do—is often blamed for people's getting into trouble.

   Idle hands are the Devil's playground.

2. Although I was very angry, I did not cause him any harm at all.

   Although I was very angry, I did not touch a hair on his head.

3. I asked Carolyn to watch my baby brother yesterday.

   I asked Carolyn to keep an eye on my baby brother yesterday.

4. In a famous scene in *Julius Caesar*, Brutus asks the citizens of Rome to listen to him.

   In a famous scene in Julius Caesar, **Brutus asks the citizens of Rome to lend him their ears.**

5. The violin section plays the opening of the composition, and then the trumpet section picks up the theme.

   The violins open the composition, and then the trumpets pick up the theme.

6. The fundraising dinner cost $200 for each plate of food.

   The fundraising dinner cost $200 a plate.

Metonymy:

7. The President of the United States and his chief advisors have asked Congress to approve an emergency tax increase.

    The White House has asked Congress to approve an emergency tax increase.

8. Go see the principal.

    Report to the office.

9. Stock brokers and investment experts hope to see gains on the market today.

    Wall Street hopes to see gains today.

10. The defense attorney requested permission to walk up to the judge to speak with him.

    The defense attorney requested permission to approach the bench.

11. Both the United States Senate and House of Representatives announced their plans to take an unprecedented three-year vacation.

    Capital Hill announced its plans to take an unprecedented three-year vacation.

11. Queen Elizabeth declared a day of mourning for victims of the earthquake.

    The crown declared a day of mourning for victims of the earthquake.

Device #28   **Hyperbaton:**

Word order, unusual but artistic...

Hyperbaton is a rhetorical device in which you arrange the words in your sentence in an unexpected order. *Hyperbaton* can tweak the normal order of a sentence to make certain parts stand out or to make the entire sentence jump off the page.

One of the most common ways to use *hyperbaton* is to put an adjective after the noun it modifies, rather than before it. While this might be a normal word order in languages like French, in English it tends to give an air of mystery to a sentence: *"The forest burned with a fire unquenchable—unquenchable except by the helicopter that finally arrived."*

Hyperbaton can also put the verb all the way at the end of the sentence, rather than between the subject and the object. So rather than, *"She wouldn't, for any reason whatsoever, be married to that smelly, foul, unlikable man,"* you could write, *"She wouldn't, for any reason whatsoever, to that smelly, foul, unlikable man, be married."* Note the force this *hyperbaton* carries with it.

You can use *hyperbaton* to separate adjectives, as well, rather than having them both before the noun. One adjective can be put in the usual place, while the other can complete the sentence, creating a nice sandwich effect around your noun. This can help separate adjectives if you want one to stand out more than the other, as in the sentence, *"It was a good idea and thoroughly unworkable."*

Hyperbaton is a bit tricky because there is no good way to explain why some uses *("Her behavior uncouth")* seem to work, while others *("Her behavior good")* sound absolutely awful. The best advice one can give is simply to try them out; err on the side of caution if you're unsure. Be aware not only of uses that seem totally ungrammatical, but also of those that come across as too stilted or overly poetic for their context. *Hyperbaton* should add a bit of flair to your writing, but it shouldn't make it absurd. If you start sounding like Yoda, you definitely have taken *hyperbaton* too far.

> *Example #1: "You have to admit it was a long year, but bearable."*

> *Example #2: "Intentions profit nothing, only promises kept matter."*

> *Example #3: "This sort of family argument necessitates a long arbitration, courtroom style."*

Exercise 1:

Write 10 original statements that are served well by using *hyperbaton*. Do not just reverse the order of words to complete the exercise.

Answers will vary.

Example:
> The baseball game, long and boring, soon put me to sleep.

1.

2.

3.

4.

5.

6.

7.

8.

9.

10.

When you see instances of *hyperbaton*, consider them conscious stylistic choices, and examine the context carefully to see why the writer has chosen to emphasize that sentence.

> *Example #1: "Bread that is fresh in the oven baked."*

> *Example #2: "'Amen,' noisily the churchgoers echoed."*

> *Example #3: "To a nunnery, go!"*

> *Example #4: "A single swallow doth not a spring make."*

ANALYSIS OF READING

Aporia:

It's possible this device should not come next, but we'll give it a try.

Aporia is a device a writer will use to express doubt about an idea. It can be used for a number of different reasons and is very valuable. At its most basic level, *aporia* serves as a way for a writer to show a number of different sides to an argument, without personally committing to any. This is the most common use of the device and also the most candid in its motives. An example of this is, *"I'm unsure whether to be in favor of harsher penalties or opposed to them, as the arguments on both sides seem very strong."*

On a more subtle level, a writer may use *aporia* to give a personal opinion on something, while appearing to express ignorance at the same time. Examples of this are sentences with the form: *"I don't know if they are aware that..."* Writers might also say they are unaware of something as a way of putting an idea into the reader's head without having to take responsibility for it—something like: *"There are those who say creating wealth, no matter who profits from it immediately, ultimately helps everyone—an idea that, while I have yet to be persuaded, seems convincing to me."*

Aporia is also sometimes used to seem to address a point, while actually dismissing it. Rather than ignore criticism or common questions, which can weaken an argument, a writer might use *aporia* to acknowledge the criticism, but then move on without any discussion of it. This is very common in political discourse, but is also seen frequently in academic writing. An example might be, *"I have heard that native deer populations in North America seem to be on the decline, and I don't know what to say about that. In my experience it seems our town is inundated by these creatures."*

As a reader, be aware of any time writers admit to not knowing something. Examine what they say afterward to see whether they act on this ignorance or whether they seem to have just paid lip service to it. Phrases to be aware of include: *"I don't know..."*; *"I cannot say..."*; *"I'm unaware of..."*; *"I often wonder..."*; *"I'm not convinced..."*; or *"I have never understood...."*

Be aware also of third-person qualifications like, *"Sources do not agree...,"* *"Experts have considerable doubt about...,"* and so on. In such constructions, the writer might just be trying to lead you into a conclusion he or she is pretending not to make.

Exercise 1:

Over the next week or so, pay attention to the newspapers, magazines, or blogs that you read. Listen closely to people you hear speaking, whether on television, radio, online, or in person. Note any uses of *aporia* you read or hear and list them. Also, decide the person's intent in using this device and evaluate the intellectual, psychological, or emotional impact the device had on you. *The first one has been done for you as an example.*

Answers will vary, but they must be valid examples of *aporia*, and the students must cite their sources and evaluate how the device functions in the text, considering both its intended impact and its actual impact.

1. Aporia: *"I'm not really certain where to begin..."*

   Impact: *Narrator is potentially unreliable. What follows might include unclear or ambiguous details.*

2. Aporia:

   Impact:

3. Aporia:

   Impact:

4. Aporia:

   Impact:

5. Aporia:

   Impact:

Exercise 2:

Use *aporia* correctly in 2 sentences about mandatory school uniforms, and be prepared to share and discuss your response with classmates.

The answers should resemble this one: "Although requiring students to wear uniforms has been shown to decrease violence and improve grades, I am not sure that such a sacrifice of individual expression and freedom is worth the positive results." Students should express both positive and negative sides of the issue. The follow-up discussion should be as calm and objective as possible, as in any mature debate.

Exercise 3:

Write a paragraph explaining how *aporia* can be both a powerful and a weak strategy in a persuasive essay, depending on how it is used.

Answers will vary but must be logical, persuasive, well written, and complete. (Note that such a paragraph will automatically include *aporia*.) For example, *aporia* can be powerful because it shows that the writer sees at least one other side to the issue; however, if overused, *aporia* can make the writer appear to be wishy-washy or unable to make definite decisions.

Device #30   ***Anaphora/Epistrophe/Symploce:***

Repeat the phrase for style. Repeat the phrase for emphasis.
Repeat the phrase for clarity. But repeat the phrase.

Anaphora is a device in which the writer repeats a word or phrase at the beginning of multiple clauses or sentences. This biblical quotation from Ecclesiastes is an excellent example of the technique: *"To every thing there is a season, and a time to every purpose under the heaven: A time to be born, and a time to die; a time to plant, and a time to pluck up that which is planted; A time to kill, and a time to heal; a time to break down, and a time to build up..."*

Epistrophe is a close relative to *anaphora*; it is one in which the same word or phrase is repeated at the end of multiple clauses or sentences. Continuing the biblical examples, the following quotation from First Corinthians is a fine illustration of *epistrophe*: *"When I was a child, I spoke as a child, I understood as a child, I thought as a child, but when I became a man, I put away childish things."*

Exercise 1:

Reword the *epistrophe* from First Chorinthians and explain why the original quotation from the Bible is more effective.

Responses will vary but should resemble this revision: "During my childhood, I spoke and reasoned the way most children do, but when I grew up, I left behind those childish traits." Students should include the basic ideas in a correct sentence with no *epistrophe*. The original version is better because it is more memorable and forceful.

Exercise 2:

Below is a passage from a very famous speech by former British Prime Minister Winston Churchill, who was a master rhetorician. Reword the passage and then explain why Churchill's original is more effective:

> ...we shall not flag or fail. We shall go on to the end, we shall fight in France, we shall fight on the seas and oceans, we shall fight with growing confidence and growing strength in the air, we shall defend our Island, whatever the cost may be, we shall fight on the beaches, we shall fight on the landing grounds, we shall fight in the fields and in the streets, we shall fight in the hills; we shall never surrender...

> Winston Churchill before the House of Commons
> June 4, 1940

Responses will vary, but should resemble this: ...we shall not flag or fail. We shall go on to the end, fighting in France, on the seas and oceans, with growing confidence and strength in the air. We shall defend our Island, whatever the cost may be. We shall fight on the beaches, on the landing grounds, in the fields and streets, in the hills. We shall never surrender...

NOTE: a student's changing "shall" to "will" or "we shall" to "we'll" does *not* meet the demands of this assignment because use of the formal or archaic "shall" or substitution of an informal contraction does not change the *anaphora*.

Exercise 3:

Take the following famous quotation and paraphrase it, *without* using *epistrophe,* while maintaining the same essential meaning. Then explain which version is better and why:

> "What lies behind us and what lies before us are tiny compared to what lies within us."—Ralph Waldo Emerson

Responses will vary but should resemble this revision: "Our individual personalities are much more important than our pasts or futures." Emerson's point, taken more deeply, is that individuals can make amends for past mistakes and can create brighter futures if their personalities are strong and positive. A revision of the quotation elaborating on that idea (e.g., "within each person is a greater ability for change than either the past or the future") is also acceptable.

As you can see, both *anaphora* and *epistrophe* act to form a sort of parallel structure that emphasizes a single idea.

Anaphora is most commonly used to build a sense of *climax.* Usually, this is done by starting with a phrase that will be repeated and ordering the clauses from least to most important. In this way, the writer guides the reader along a very clear path, with a clearly demarcated end. For example, *"We look in toward the Milky Way, in toward the system of Sol, in toward the planet Earth, in toward the nation of China, and, finally, in toward a lonely hut on a lonely hill."*

Epistrophe has a somewhat similar purpose. By ending each clause with the same word or phrase, that phrase is emphasized each time. In effect, the phrase becomes a sort of punctuation mark, which the reader can expect to find each time. *Epistrophe* is a bit trickier for writers to use without sounding overblown, but when used correctly, it is an effective form of emphasis. For example, *"In old age we laugh at our past, sigh for our past, cry out over our past."*

A special form, called *symploce,* combines both *anaphora* and *epistrophe.* Although this sounds as if it would be rarely used, *symploce* is actually not that uncommon in formal writing. The total parallelism it forms creates a feeling of completion as well as emphasis. For example, *"We enjoy life when we know ourselves to be free of temptation and sin, but we enjoy life also when we give ourselves completely to temptation and sin."*

Exercise 4:

Write 10 original statements that use *anaphora, epistrophe,* or *symploce*. *The first one has been done for you as an example.*

1. *We played the game, we played hard, we played as if our lives depended on it, we played as if our entire family's lives hung in the balance, but we lost.*

2.

3.

4.

5.

6.

7.

8.

9.

10.

11.

All of these devices should be easy to recognize, since their form is simple and obvious. Any time an important word or phrase is repeated at the beginning or end of consecutive phrases or sentences, pay careful attention to the word or phrase being repeated. Both *anaphora* and *epistrophe* are writers' ways of planting flags on concepts that they want you to especially note.

Exercise 5:

Underline the examples of *anaphora* in Lincoln's Gettysburg Address.

Four score and seven years ago our fathers brought forth on this continent a new nation, conceived in liberty and dedicated to the proposition that all men are created equal. Now we are engaged in a great civil war, testing whether that nation or any nation so conceived and so dedicated can long endure. We are met on a great battlefield of that war. We have come to dedicate a portion of that field as a final resting-place for those who here gave their lives that that nation might live. It is altogether fitting and proper that we should do this. But, in a larger sense, <u>we cannot dedicate, we cannot consecrate, we cannot hallow</u> this ground. The brave men, living and dead, who struggled here have consecrated it far above our poor power to add or detract. The world will little note nor long remember what we say here, but it can never forget what they did here. <u>It is for us the living, rather, to be dedicated here</u> to the unfinished work which they who fought here have thus far so nobly advanced. <u>It is rather for us to be here dedicated</u> to the great task remaining before us—<u>that</u> from these honored dead we take increased devotion to that cause for which they gave the last full measure of devotion—<u>that</u> we here highly resolve that these dead shall not have died in vain, <u>that</u> this nation under God shall have a new birth of freedom, and <u>that</u> government of the people, by the people, for the people shall not perish from the earth.

The first instance of *anaphora* is obvious; the next two may be questioned or missed by students. The second instance is not an exact *anaphora*, but it is enough of a repetition to be in the spirit of an *anaphora* and to make use of the device's *rhetorical* power. The third instance is strictly correct (the repetition of the word "that"), and you can also note that the sentence structure is nearly identical after each use of "that," making the *parallelism* even more effective.

Amplification:

This is an important device—more than mere repetition—it's an actual expansion of the information already given.

In *amplification*, writers repeat something they've just said, while adding more detail and information to the original description. *Amplification* is not only a good strategic device, but also adds style to the phrase it amplifies. For example, *"Next we come to the fruit fly—the drosophila melanogaster, that tiny, insubstantial bug, on whom the foundations of biology have rested for so long."*

The main purpose of *amplification* is to focus the reader's attention on an idea he or she might otherwise miss. Writers might add a small amount of *amplification* to an idea, or a larger, sometimes prolific, amount. The amount added depends on a number of factors: details the writer actually wants to convey, how important the idea is, or how likely it is that it will be skimmed over. Often, to a reader, these details will seem entirely unneeded, but that's because the purpose is not to inform, but to emphasize, such as, *"It was a cold day, a wicked day, a day of biting winds and bitter frost."*

The preceding information is not to say that details given in *amplification* will never be important. If you find yourself wondering, however, why a writer has devoted so much attention to giving details that seem to have no relevance, consider the possibility that he or she simply wants you to remember the idea itself. Writers have limited tools at their disposal to convey emphasis. Unlike the spoken word, in which intonation lets us know what is and is not important, on the page, sentence construction is all we have. Devices like *amplification* allow writers to emphasize an idea without it feeling too heavy-handed to the reader. For example, *"Look to the genome for our future, a future free of disease and decay."*

Exercise 1:

Analyze a chapter from your history, science, or any other textbook. Identify 3 helpful uses of *amplification*, and 3 uses that appear to have minimal effect for the reader. Explain each instance's usefulness, or lack thereof.

The first one has been done for you as an example.

Answers will vary, but they must be valid examples of *amplification*, and the student must provide a full and reasonable explanation of the usefulness of the expansion.

Helpful

1. **Amplification:** *"The Earth's climate has indeed changed over time—time that is measured in eons rather than years."*

    Explanation: *The amplification here is helpful because it emphasizes the vastness of geologic time compared to human time.*

2. **Amplification:**

    Explanation:

3. **Amplification:**

    Explanation:

4. **Amplification:**

    Explanation:

Minimal

1. **Amplification:** *The United States in a nation of laws, laws that protect the rights of the individual.*

    Explanation: *This repetition of "law" is less effective because it adds no real emphasis to the explanation that follows.*

2. **Amplification:**

    Explanation:

3. **Amplification:**

    Explanation:

4. **Amplification:**

    Explanation:

Exercise 2:

"Some people seem to succeed in life without goals or plans. However, without goals or plans, success is very hard to achieve because it depends on chance, on what other people do, and on having excellent judgment as to what decisions to make at any given time." Explain why this use of *amplification* is effective or ineffective. Be specific and logical in your reasoning and be prepared to discuss your opinion with the rest of the class.

This example is effective because it fits the definition of *amplification* and offers three logical reasons why success would be hard without having goals or plans. In fact, it may be pointed out that the sentence would make a good thesis for an essay on the subject. One criticism, however, may be that very long sentences may weaken the effect.

Exercise 3:

Provide *amplification* for the following statements by American psychologist William James.

Answers will vary but should be logically connected, grammatically correct, and good examples of *amplification*. Below are some suggested responses.

1. "In the practical use of our intellect, forgetting is as important as remembering."

   How practical would it be to remember everything and forget nothing? Our brains would be so cluttered with the unnecessary and the painful that we could not function.

2. "The greatest discovery of any generation is that a human being can alter his life by altering his attitude."

   After all, attitude is the most important part of living: one's attitude determines how one perceives, makes decisions, and achieves success or suffers failure.

3. "A great many people think they are thinking when they are rearranging their prejudices."

   Although the rearrangement of thoughts and ideas is a part of thinking, it is not progress in thinking. Maintaining prejudices means that a person does not try to understand and embrace alternatives, choosing instead to think within preset boundaries.

4. "My first act of free will shall be to believe in free will."

   For what is freedom without action and belief? If one is free but decides to do nothing about it, what difference does freedom make in one's life? Having free will implies the need to use it.

Device #32   **Personification:**

Your writing will spring to life and energize your readers with fire-breathing ideas.

Personification is the act of giving human attributes to something that is non-human. It might be an animal, an inanimate object, or an abstract concept. A leader interested in spreading democracy might use *personification* like this: *"We expect freedom to spread its wings across the globe and allow oppressed people to enjoy its warmth."* Personification is widely used, and as a result, there are a number of clichés one sees everywhere—for example, *"The wind whistles in the trees."* The best *personifications*, however, are immediately understood without resorting to familiar clichés—for example, *"The wind gently swept through the valley and slipped in through the cracks in the barn."*

By using *personification*, writers are trying to help the reader understand particular qualities of whatever they're writing about. Rather than try to explain it in abstract terms, the writer can rely on the common human experience to describe what is meant. Since we are all familiar with human characteristics and human emotions, *personification* gives us a starting point to better understand whatever the writer is trying to convey, such as in this example: *"The cool wind gently bathed the runner's hot and tired body."*

Often, *personification* seems so natural that we don't even notice it. Many inanimate objects are described in human terms so regularly that it seems as if they actually possess these attributes. It's only when we stop to think about it that we realize a lawnmower can't really be finicky or stubborn, and the actual office we're working in can't be friendly, compatible, healthy, etc. These human emotions, however, immediately let us know something about the situation. They do it without having to explain that the lawnmower sometimes starts and sometimes doesn't, or that an office space has good lighting and isn't cluttered.

When you encounter adjectives that describe human emotions, but are not tied to a human, think about why the writer might have used non-literal terms. Why did the writer choose to describe the sunlight as "cheerful," (light cannot literally be cheerful or otherwise), rather than as "bright," which it can be? In this case, it is done so the author can allow the reader to bring some personal interpretation to the sentence. Your idea of "cheerful" is different from someone else's, and when coupled with an inanimate object like "sunshine," each reader comes up with slightly altered nuances in meaning.

Personification isn't limited to adjectives, as in this example *"I like my steak so raw it gets up and tries to walk away."* As we can see, inanimate objects or abstract concepts might also perform actions in writing that they never could in the real world, such as, *"I'm usually not a fan of gospel music, but that choir could really sing—the pews themselves were clapping their hands and stomping their feet."* Writing often has objects singing, howling, dancing, performing acts that are impossible, however, as in, *"My heart sings when I see your face,"* or *"Blind justice wept the day Sam Roberts was acquitted for the crime everyone knew he had committed."*

Exercise 1:

Read the following poem and underline each instance of *personification*. Then, briefly describe the effect of *personification* on the poem's meaning.

Two <u>**Sunflowers**</u>
<u>**Move**</u> in the Yellow Room.
(William Blake)

"Ah, William, <u>**we're weary**</u> of weather,"
said the sunflowers, shining with dew.
"Our <u>traveling habits</u> have <u>tired</u> us.
Can you give us a room with a view?"

They arranged themselves at the window
and <u>counted</u> the steps of the sun,
and they both took root in the carpet
where the topaz tortoises <u>run</u>.

Answers will vary. Example: Blake describes the possible thoughts of two sunflowers that he has rescued from the outdoors. His use of *personification* allows the reader to "hear the flowers' thoughts" and see their "actions." In this use of *personification*, the flowers "speak for themselves."

Note that "both took root" is not an example of *personification* because plants usually perform this activity on their own—it is not a human characteristic. "Run" is an example of *personification* because it relates to the "topaz tortoises," a design that is "in the carpet." Tortoises cannot actually run.

Exercise 2:

Take this ordinary paragraph and make it "come alive" through your use of *personification*. Obviously, not all the ideas or inanimate objects are suitable for *personification*, but many are.

Answers will vary. Opportunities exist in the paragraph for numerous uses of *personification*—at least every sentence has the possibility. Encourage the students not to put *personification* in each sentence, however, which would make their paragraphs seem too forced.

What a horrible morning it was! Mondays were usually difficult, but this particular morning was the worst. I could barely struggle out of the covers. My muscles felt weak, and my lower back hurt. Sunday, I had worked in the garden pulling weeds all afternoon under the blazing sun. Somehow, crabgrass had covered most of the soil where my vegetables were to be. The weeds were tough to pull out, and it took a three-pronged rake to get them loose. Next year—no garden!

Device #33   ***Parataxis:***

Think of a topic, jot down your ideas, write your essay.

Parataxis involves listing a series of clauses with no conjunctions, as in this example: "My dad went to Las Vegas, he lost his money, he came home." Although similar to asyndeton, parataxis must relate to clauses.

Parataxis often implies a sense of immediacy, indicating multiple things happening at once, even though that may not be the case. One of the more famous examples of *parataxis* is Julius Caesar's comment, *"I came, I saw, I conquered."* Typically, *parataxis* involves short, concise sentences, as the lack of conjunctions can make longer sentences difficult to understand. When you see a series of unrelated clauses listed without a conjunction, examine them carefully to see what sort of conclusion the author might be leading you to, or what effect he or she is trying to create. For example, *"We walked, we ate, we made merry in the streets,"* and *"The coat was a riot of color: green, blue, red, yellow, orange, purple, pink."* The first conveys a rush of seemingly concurrent actions and the second a combination of colors, jumbling together.

Often, *parataxis* is used to set a scene. It may also imply a series of events or moods to the reader without spelling them out, such as, *"We sat on the porch, listening to the silence of the evening: the whispering breeze in the tall grass, the crickets chirping, doves cooing, waves lapping, the terrified scream of a woman on the dock."*

Exercise 1:

Over the next week or so, pay attention to the newspapers, magazines, or blogs that you read. Listen closely to people you hear speaking, whether on television, radio, online, or in person. Note any uses of *parataxis* you encounter and list them. Also, decide the person's intent in using this device and evaluate the intellectual, psychological, or emotional impact they had on you. *The first one has been done for you as an example.*

Answers will vary.

1. Parataxis: *Attorneys for both sides cited the facts that neither of the defendants was seen dancing with the girl, that both passed polygraph exams, that no forensic evidence has been discovered to link the defendants to the crime.*

   Source: *Crime Beat*

   Intent: *Emphasize the number of facts both agree on.*

   Impact: *Casts doubt on the strength of the Prosecution's case.*

2. Parataxis:

   Source:

   Intent:

   Impact:

3. Parataxis:

   Source:

   Intent:

   Impact:

4. Parataxis:

   Source:

   Intent:

   Impact:

5. Parataxis:
    Source:
    Intent:
    Impact:

6. Parataxis:
    Source:
    Intent:
    Impact:

7. Parataxis:
    Source:
    Intent:
    Impact:

8. Parataxis:
    Source:
    Intent:
    Impact:

9. Parataxis:
    Source:
    Intent:
    Impact:

10. Parataxis:
    Source:
    Intent:
    Impact:

CUMULATIVE EXERCISES

Cumulative Exercises I:

Passages #1, #2, and #3 make use of many of the rhetorical devices that you have studied. Passage #1 includes *Climax*, *Anadiplosis*, *Parenthesis*, *Apostrophe*, *Analogy*, and *Enumeratio*. There are other devices in the passage, but concentrate on identifying these. Underline and try to identify each device used; then explain why the excerpt you chose illustrates it. Some sentences may have more than one device, so read the entire passage carefully. List your choices in the places supplied after each passage.

Passage #1:

The Colorado River begins as a relatively unremarkable river, flowing southwest through Colorado and Utah. It grows slowly but steadily throughout its journey, and by the time it hits Marble Canyon in Arizona it is up to 2,000 feet wide and 130 feet deep. At the end of Marble Canyon, it is joined by the Little Colorado River, turning the original placidly moving water into a raging beast of a river. It is then that it begins to wend its way through its greatest achievement: the Grand Canyon.

"The Grand Canyon" is a name that, were it given to any other geologic formation, would seem overblown. When compared with the actual physical presence, however, the name seems scarcely to describe it. There are no words to describe the wonder (and wonder does not do it justice) of the Grand Canyon. Bear with me then, gentle reader, as I try to put words to the ineffable, to describe this wound of the divine, this chasm that cannot be, this Grand Canyon. The Grand Canyon is immense—fifteen miles wide at points, over a mile deep, spanning two hundred seventy-seven miles, exposing over two billion years of history to our eager eyes.

Since it was first viewed by a European in the mid-1500s, the Grand Canyon has captivated the hearts and imaginations of people across the globe. It attracts more than five million visitors each year and is often said to be one of the few things in life that does not disappoint when you finally experience it. Upon first viewing the canyon, many people find it difficult to take it in. It simply seems too large to be possible—like trying to understand the scope of the universe, or to contemplate eternity. It is only after a few days of hiking its myriad trails, of sleeping beneath its stars, and of having one's soul soothed by the ceaseless Colorado River that one begins to understand. Like eternity, like the universe itself, the Grand Canyon lets us touch the greater mystery of life, and come away fundamentally changed.

1. Device: *climax*
   Excerpt: **The Colorado River begins as a relatively unremarkable river, flowing southwest through Colorado and Utah. It grows slowly but steadily throughout its journey, and by the time it hits Marble Canyon in Arizona it is up to 2000' wide and 130' deep. At the end of Marble Canyon, it is joined by the Little Colorado River, turning the original placidly moving water into a raging beast of a river. It is then that it begins to wend its way through its greatest achievement: the Grand Canyon.**

   Explanation:

2. Device: *parenthesis*
   Excerpt: **There are no words to describe the wonder (and wonder does not do it justice) of the Grand Canyon.**

   Explanation:

3. Device: *apostrophe*
   Excerpt: **bear with me then, gentle reader**

   Explanation:

4. Device: *anadiplosis*
    Excerpt: **This Grand Canyon. The Grand Canyon**

    Explanation:

5. Device: *enumeratio*
    Excerpt: **The ineffable, to describe this wound of the
                       divine, this chasm that cannot be, this Grand
                       Canyon.**

    Explanation:

6. Device: *analogy*
    Excerpt: **Like trying to understand the scope of the
                       universe, or to contemplate eternity.**

    Explanation:

Passage #2 includes *Chiasmus, Conduplicatio, Antanagoge, Parenthesis,* and *Asyndeton*. There are other devices in the passage, but concentrate on identifying these. Underline and try to identify each device used; then explain why the excerpt you chose illustrates it. Some sentences may have more than one device, so read the entire passage carefully. List your choices in the places supplied after each passage.

Passage #2:

Since the advent of the personal computer and the Internet in the latter part of the 20th century, the face of the world has been drastically changed. <u>Banking, shopping, research, communication</u>—all are now handled online by many people.

<u>Let us look not on the darker side of this technology—truly all creations have the potential for ill as well as good. Instead, let us see</u> in it the limitless possibility it offers. Greater than the printing press, greater than the telegraph or the telephone, the Internet is one of humankind's crowning achievements. The Internet offers all people the opportunity to learn about events throughout the world, to research upcoming elections and candidates—<u>and in ways beyond counting</u>—to expand their own horizons.

In practice, however, the innumerable benefits offered by the Internet are available only to those who can afford a computer and an Internet connection. It is an unjust situation, and one that should not be allowed to exist in our modern world. <u>Access to the tools of liberty—like liberty itself—must be a basic human right. We must endeavor to provide free access terminals anywhere and everywhere, to ensure that liberty</u> remains the province of the many, and not the few.

The cost of such an undertaking will no doubt be great. While libraries have assumed some of this burden, a truly equitable solution must involve far greater resources being committed. It will tax us both literally and figuratively. But the benefits far outweigh these petty costs: the ability for all to function fully in a global community; the possibility for more advanced, more truly democratic political procedures, made possible only through the use of the Internet; the establishment once more of America as a place where no one is cast out into the cold. Against such benefits, what cost could be too great?

1. Device: *asyndeton*
    Excerpt: **banking, shopping, research, communication**

    Explanation:

2. Device: *antanagoge*
    Excerpt: **Let us look not on the darker side of this
                    technology—truly all creations have the
                    potential for ill as well as good.**

    Explanation:

3. Device: *parenthesis*
    Excerpt: **—and in ways beyond counting—**

    Explanation:

4. Device: *conduplicatio*
    Excerpt: **Access to the tools of liberty—like liberty
                    itself—must be a basic human right. We must
                    endeavor to provide free access terminals
                    anywhere and everywhere, to ensure that
                    liberty**

    Explanation:

5. Device: *chiasmus*
    Excerpt: **Let us look not... Instead, let us see**

    Explanation:

Passage #3 includes *Sententia, Exemplum, Analogy/Simile, Personification, Anaphora/Epistrophe, Amplification, Aporia,* and *Metaphor.* There are other devices in the passage, but concentrate on identifying these. Underline and try to identify each device used; then explain why the excerpt you chose illustrates it. Some sentences may have more than one device, so read the entire passage carefully. List your choices in the places supplied after each passage.

Passage #3:

A wise man once said, "War is hell." And perhaps no war exemplifies this sentiment as well as the conflict that took place in Southeast Asia between 1959 and 1975. In those 16 years, more than 58,000 Americans were killed, and as many as five million Vietnamese died. We lived, we breathed, we died in the shadow of this conflict. What is not as often spoken of in regards to Vietnam is the horror visited upon the other inhabitants of Indochina. For example, during this same time frame more than 700,000 Cambodians were killed, and the groundwork was set for the mass genocide that was to come.

Cambodia was like the woman wandering obliviously across a field while a crazed bull charged at a distant target. Caught in the middle of a conflict in which she had no part, her people nonetheless paid an incredible price. The innocence of this gentle nation was ravished during the War in Indochina, and it is a testament to the resiliency of her people that they, for the most part, do not hold Americans responsible for their fate.

Traveling today in Cambodia, one is constantly faced with reminders of the War in Indochina and the subsequent horrors of the Khmer Rouge. Signs warning of land mine danger dot the countryside, and the victims of these long-slumbering mines are everywhere—missing eyes, arms, and legs, rolling on improvised skateboards, or playing in makeshift bands to earn enough money to survive for another day.

I do not know if we Americans deserve the kindness the Cambodian people show us. I do not know if we will ever wash clean the blood from our hands, or live down the shame of what we have done. I only know that I look to the Cambodian people for inspiration. <u>They are beacons of light</u>, shining with grace, forgiveness, and a strength unshakable. When I stumble at the cruelty of this sometimes harsh world, I turn my mind to thoughts of these people, and their example helps me to my feet once more.

1. Device: *sententia*
    Excerpt: **"War is hell."**

    Explanation:

2. Device: *exemplum*
    Excerpt: **No war exemplifies this sentiment as well as the conflict that took place in Southeast Asia between 1959 and 1975.**

    Explanation:

3. Device: *anaphora/epistrophe*
    Excerpt: **We lived, we breathed, we died in the shadow of this conflict.**

    Explanation:

4. Device: *analogy/simile*
    Excerpt: **Cambodia was like the woman wandering obliviously across a field while a crazed bull charged at a distant target.**

    Explanation:

5. Device: *amplification*

    Excerpt: **Traveling today in Cambodia, one is constantly faced with reminders of the War in Indochina and the subsequent horrors of the Khmer rouge. Signs warning of land mine danger dot the countryside, and the victims of these long-slumbering mines are everywhere—missing eyes, arms, and legs, rolling on improvised skateboards, or playing in makeshift bands to earn enough money to survive for another day.**

    Explanation:

6. Device: *metaphor*

    Excerpt: **they are beacons of light**

    Explanation:

7. Device: *aporia*

    Excerpt: **I do not know if we Americans deserve the kindness the Cambodian people show us. I do not know if we will ever**

    Explanation:

8. Device: *personification*

    Excerpt: **The innocence of this gentle nation**

    Explanation:

Cumulative Exercises II:

Passages #4, #5, and #6 make additional use of some of the rhetorical devices that you have studied. Passage #4 includes *Anaphora, Allusion, Simile,* and *Metaphor.* There are other devices in the passage, but concentrate on identifying these. Underline and try to identify each device used; then explain why the excerpt you chose illustrates it, why each device is used, and what each contributes to the overall purpose, meaning, and effect of the passage. Some sentences may have more than one device, so read the entire passage carefully. List your choices in the places supplied after each passage.

Passage #4:

<u>Art is what truly separates us from the animals. Art is our highest calling, and greatest achievement. Art is that which allows us to transcend earthly life and commune with the divine. And art</u> is being stripped on a daily basis from our schools in favor of more and more mathematics and hard sciences.

There are those who argue that art is a decadent luxury in this modern age. They would argue that in an increasingly competitive world, our students must spend as much time and energy as is possible on math and science if they are to survive; but do we not also need beauty to survive? Does not the ability to translate our world creatively help us to survive? And what life is it we have saved for ourselves when we rob it of art?

It is no doubt true that math and science play a greater and greater role in the workplace, and it is reasonable to devote no small amount of attention to their instruction. But, it seems equally apparent that the arts should not suffer as collateral damage. Those who fail to see their importance have likely never felt their grace. <u>Like some sort of anti-Prometheus, they would steal the fire that has made us great.</u>

Math and the sciences may be the brain of our collective self, but art is the heart. <u>Art is like beauty</u>—it may appear to have no purpose, but ultimately, it drives us to greater heights and greater achievements. We will have failed a significant test when we allow art to be stripped from our curriculum. We may yet <u>swallow that</u>

<u>bitter pill</u> for the illusory competitive edge, but future generations will look back on that decision, shake their heads, and wonder how we could have let such things be.

1. Device: ***anaphora***
    Excerpt: **Art is what truly separates us from the animals. Art is our highest calling, and greatest achievement. Art is that which allows us to transcend earthly life and commune with the divine. And art...**

    Explanation:

2. Device: ***allusion***
    Excerpt: **Like some sort of Anti-Prometheus, they would steal the fire that has made us great.**

    Explanation:

3. Device: ***simile***
    Excerpt: **Art is like beauty**

    Explanation:

4. Device: ***metaphor***
    Excerpt: **swallow that bitter pill**

    Explanation:

Passage #5 includes *Epithet, Asyndeton, Allusion, Metaphor, Simile,* and *Synecdoche*. There are other devices in the passage, but concentrate on identifying these. Underline and try to identify each device used; then explain why the excerpt you chose illustrates it, why each device is used, and what each contributes to the overall purpose, meaning, and effect of the passage. Some sentences may have more than one device, so read the entire passage carefully. List your choices in the places supplied after each passage.

Passage #5:

In 1896, the first modern Olympic games were held, with 200 athletes competing in nine different sports: <u>**track and field, cycling, swimming, equestrian, shooting, weightlifting, wrestling, gymnastics, fencing**</u>. Fencing, the art of the blade, the sport of war, physical chess, had a long and noble tradition before its inclusion in the Olympic games, but the new athletic focus and international recognition helped transform it from the purview of duels and soldiers into a modern sport.

Fencing dates back thousands of years, with carvings in Egypt dating from 1200 B.C., showing a bout being fought with masks and protective gear. The Greeks and Romans both had their own brand of fencing as well, though it can seem barbaric and heavy-handed in comparison to modern forms. It wasn't until the 15th century that what we think of as fencing began to truly take form, with <u>**silvery blades and catlike grace**</u> taking precedence over brute strength. The great fencing masters of the day, from Agrippa to Vigiani to St. Didier, laid out principles of form and footwork still used to this day.

It is often said that <u>**fencing is like chess at one hundred miles an hour**</u>, a reference to the combination of athleticism and sophisticated strategy used. Fencing requires profound fitness of body, keenness of intellect, and strength of heart. Modern fencers practice for hours each day, conditioning their bodies to the highest level and studying strategy and theory endlessly. They must be as <u>**Sisyphus**</u>, plodding endlessly against seemingly impossible odds to achieve greatness.

All <u>Olympians are gods</u> among men. Fencers, it seems however, wear this godhead with a particular grace and poise. Perhaps it is <u>the romanticism of the blade</u>, perhaps the particular blend of form and lightning-fast reflexes they cultivate, perhaps a simple fascination with refined violence. It is difficult to dispute, however, that there is a special sort of thrill to be had from watching the blade streak through the air, and hearing that first report of steel on steel.

For more than 110 years, fencing has been an integral part of the Olympic games, and although the sport has faced its share of hardships—evolving technologies, difficulties in accurate judging, and a sometimes fickle public—it seems likely that fencing will remain at the heart of the Olympics for years to come.

1. Device: *asyndeton*
   Excerpt: **track and field, cycling, swimming, equestrian, shooting, weightlifting, wrestling, gymnastics, fencing**

   Explanation:

2. Device: *epithet*
   Excerpt: **silvery blades and catlike grace**

   Explanation:

3. Device: *simile*
   Excerpt: **fencing is like chess at one hundred miles an hour**

   Explanation:

4. Device: *allusion*
    Excerpt: **Sisyphus**

    Explanation:

5. Device: *metaphor*
    Excerpt: **Olympians are gods**

    Explanation:

6. Device: *synecdoche*
    Excerpt: **The romanticism of the blade**

    Explanation:

Passage #6 includes *Conduplicatio, Hyperbaton, Polysyndeton*, and *Metonymy*. There are other devices in the passage, but concentrate on identifying these. Underline and try to identify each device used; then explain why the excerpt you chose illustrates it, why each device is used, and what each contributes to the overall purpose, meaning, and effect of the passage. Some sentences may have more than one device, so read the entire passage carefully. List your choices in the places supplied after each passage.

Passage #6:

In the 20th century, there are countless examples of greed and power run amok, ruining the lives of innocents throughout the world. Some of the most poignant come from the so-called "banana republics," and, in particular, the nation of Honduras. The story of the United Fruit Company and its dealings in Honduras is one of <u>intrigue and double-dealing and vicious murders and theft</u> on a grand scale.

Throughout the 1800s, the United States and American businessmen held considerable control in Honduras. By owning railroads, large amounts of land, and mining operations throughout the country, they were able to wield more power than many government officials. <u>At the turn of the 20th century, these companies—and the United Fruit Company in particular—began expanding and centralizing their power. By 1929, the United Fruit Company controlled more than 650,000 acres of the best land in Honduras.</u>

Throughout the 1930s banana-producing regions in Honduras were run like small Dukedoms, with corporate-dukes ruling over them with an <u>iron fist</u>, exercising complete control. Bananas would eventually come to represent nearly 90% of Honduras' exports, making the nation entirely dependent on the beneficence of the American corporate-dukes and their commercial interests. These <u>Rockefellers</u> were able to influence government policy so absolutely that they became the *de facto* rulers of the nation. The United States government trained the Honduran army and air force, and then placed these forces under the command of US officers. <u>The resulting army existed almost exclusively for the interests of the banana companies to protect.</u>

Throughout the 1960s, in spite of returning small bits of land to the government as an overture of reconciliation, the fruit companies continued to dominate the nation. In the aftermath of hurricanes in the 1970s, their production went down drastically, and their stranglehold on the nation was lessened, further decreasing through the 1980s. As the fruit companies pulled out, however, the US military began to fill the power vacuum, transforming huge parts of the nation into US military bases.

Honduras today remains <u>shaped drastically</u> by its long history of subjugation to US business interests. So it is that the term "banana republic"—used to perfectly describe this poor nation's fate—has become the phrase of choice in describing a complete loss of power combined with a dependence on US support.

1. Device: *polysyndeton*
    Excerpt: **intrigue and double-dealing and vicious murders and theft**

    Explanation:

2. Device: *conduplicatio*
    Excerpt: **at the turn of the 20th century, these companies—and the United Fruit Company in particular—began expanding and centralizing their power. By 1929, the United Fruit Company controlled more than 650,000 acres of the best land in Honduras.**

    Explanation:

3. Device: *metonymy*
   Excerpt: **iron fist; Rockefellers**

   Explanation:

4. Device: *hyperbaton*
   Excerpt: **The resulting army existed almost exclusively for the interests of the banana companies to protect; shaped drastically**

   Explanation:

Cumulative Exercise III:

What follows is the inaugural address of President John F. Kennedy, delivered on January 20, 1961. President Kennedy was famous for his speeches, which were both intellectually challenging and emotionally moving. Thirty incidents of effective rhetorical usage are shown to you. Try to identify the devices, and state how effective they might have been in influencing the listener.

Inaugural Address of President John F, Kennedy, January 20, 1961

We observe today not **(1)** <u>a victory of party, but a celebration of freedom</u>, **(2)** <u>symbolizing an end as well as a beginning, signifying renewal, as well as change</u>. For I have sworn before you and Almighty God the same solemn oath our forebears prescribed nearly a century and three-quarters ago.

The world is very different now. For man holds in his mortal hands the power to abolish **(3)** <u>all forms of human poverty and all forms of human life.</u> And yet the same revolutionary beliefs for which our forebears fought are still at issue around the globe—the belief that the rights of man come **(4)** <u>not from the generosity of the state, but from the hand of God</u>.

We dare not forget today that we are the heirs of that first revolution. Let the word go forth from this time and place, to friend and foe alike, that the **(5)** <u>torch has been passed</u> to a new generation of Americans—**(6)** <u>born in this century, tempered by war, disciplined by a hard and bitter peace, proud of our ancient heritage</u>—and unwilling to witness or permit the slow undoing of those human rights to which this nation has always been committed, and to which we are committed today at home and around the world. Let every nation know, whether it wishes us well or ill, that **(7)** <u>we shall pay any price, bear any burden, meet any hardship, support any friend, oppose any foe</u> to assure the survival and the success of liberty.

This much we pledge—and more. To those old allies whose cultural and spiritual origins we share, we pledge the loyalty of faithful friends. **(8)** <u>United, there is little we cannot do in a host of cooperative ventures. Divided, there is little we can do</u> for we dare not meet a powerful challenge at odds and split asunder.

To those new States whom we welcome to the ranks of the free, we pledge our word that one form of colonial control shall not have passed away merely to be replaced by a far more iron tyranny. **(9)** <u>We shall not always expect to find them supporting our view.</u> <u>But we shall always</u> hope to find them strongly supporting their own freedom—and to remember that, in the past, those who foolishly sought power by **(10)** <u>riding the back of the tiger</u> ended up inside. To those people in the huts and villages across the globe struggling to break the bonds of mass misery, we pledge our best efforts **(11)** <u>to help them help themselves,</u> for whatever period is required—**(12)** <u>not because the Communists may be doing it, not because we seek their votes, but because</u> it is right. **(13)** <u>If a free society cannot help the many who are poor, it cannot save the few who are rich</u>.

To our sister republics south of our border, we offer a special pledge: to convert **(14)** <u>our good words into good deeds</u> in a new alliance for progress, to assist **(15)** <u>free men and free governments</u> in casting off **(16)** <u>the chains of poverty</u>. But this peaceful **(17)** <u>revolution of hope</u> cannot become the prey of hostile powers. Let all our neighbors know that we shall join with them to oppose aggression or subversion anywhere in the Americas.

And let every other power know that this hemisphere intends to remain the **(18)** <u>master of its own house</u>.

To that world assembly of sovereign states, the United Nations, our last best hope in an age where the **(19)** <u>instruments of war have far outpaced the instruments of peace</u>, we renew our pledge of support—to prevent it from becoming merely a forum for invective—to strengthen its shield of the new and the weak—and to enlarge the area in which its writ may run. Finally, to those nations who would make themselves our adversary, we offer not a pledge but a request: that both sides begin anew the quest for peace—before the dark powers of destruction unleashed by science engulf all humanity in planned or accidental self-destruction. We dare not tempt them with weakness. For only when our arms are **(20)** <u>sufficient beyond doubt can we be certain beyond doubt</u> that they will never be employed. But neither can two great and powerful groups of nations take comfort from our present course—both sides overburdened by the cost of modern weapons, both rightly alarmed by the steady spread of the deadly atom, yet both racing to alter that uncertain balance of terror that stays the hand of mankind's final war. So let us begin anew—remembering on both sides that civility is not a sign of weakness, and sincerity is always subject to proof.

(21) Let us never negotiate out of fear. But let us never fear to negotiate. **(22)** Let both sides explore what problems unite us instead of belaboring those problems which divide us. **(23-1)** Let both sides, for the first time, formulate serious and precise proposals for the inspection and control of arms—and bring the **(24)** absolute power to destroy other nations under the absolute control of all nations. **(23-2)** Let both sides seek to invoke the wonders of science instead of its terrors. Together let us **(25)** explore the stars, conquer the deserts, eradicate disease, tap the ocean depths and encourage the arts and commerce. **(23-3)** Let both sides unite to heed, in all corners of the earth, the command of Isaiah—to "undo the heavy burdens...and to let the oppressed go free." And if a **(26)** beachhead of cooperation may push back the jungle of suspicion, let both sides join in creating a new endeavor—not a new balance of power, but a new world of law—**(27)** where the strong are just and the weak secure and the peace preserved. **(28)** All this will not be finished in the first one hundred days. Nor will it be finished in the first one thousand days; nor in the life of this Administration; nor even perhaps in our lifetime on this planet. But let us begin. In your hands, my fellow citizens, more than mine, will rest the final success or failure of our course. Since this country was founded, each generation of Americans has been summoned to give testimony to its national loyalty. The graves of young Americans who answered the call to service surround the globe. Now the trumpet summons us again—**(29)** not as a call to bear arms, though arms we need—not as a call to battle, though embattled we are—but a call to bear the burden of a long twilight struggle, year in and year out, rejoicing in hope, patient in tribulation, a struggle against the common enemies of man: tyranny, poverty, disease, and war itself.

Can we forge against these enemies a grand and global alliance, North and South, East and West, that can assure a more fruitful life for all mankind? Will you join in that historic effort? In the long history of the world, only a few generations have been granted the role of defending freedom in its hour of maximum danger. I do not shrink from this responsibility—I welcome it. I do not believe that any of us would exchange places with any other people or any other generation. The energy, the faith, the devotion which we bring to this endeavor will light our country and all who serve it—and the glow from that fire can truly light the world. And so, my fellow Americans: ask not what your country can do for you; ask what you can do for your country. My fellow citizens of the world: (30) <u>ask not what America will do for you, but what together we can do for the freedom of man.</u>

Finally, whether you are citizens of America or citizens of the world, ask of us here the same high standards of strength and sacrifice which we ask of you. With a good conscience our only sure reward, with history the final judge of our deeds, let us go forth to lead the land we love, asking His blessing and His help, but knowing that here on earth God's work must truly be our own.

1. Device: ***antithesis***
   Impact:

2. Device: ***parallelism***
   Impact:

3. Device: ***anaphora***
   Impact:

4. Device: ***antithesis***
   Impact:

5. Device: *metaphor*
   Impact:

6. Device: *parallelism*
   Impact:

7. Device: *parallelism*
   Impact:

8. Device: *antithesis*
   Impact:

9. Device: *anaphora*
   Impact:

10. Device: *metaphor/allusion*
    Impact:

11. Device: *conduplicatio*
    Impact:

12. Device: *anaphora*
    Impact:

13. Device: *parallelism*
    Impact:

14. Device: *conduplicatio*
    Impact:

15. Device: *conduplicatio*
    Impact:

16. Device: *metaphor*
    Impact:

17. Device: *metaphor*
    Impact:

18. Device: *metaphor*
    Impact:

19. Device: *conduplicatio*
    Impact:

20. Device: *parallelism*
    Impact:

21. Device: *chiasmus*
    Impact:

22. Device: *antithesis*
    Impact:

23. Device: *anaphora*
    Impact:

24. Device: *conduplicatio*
    Impact:

25. Device: *asyndeton*
    Impact:

26. Device: *metaphor*
    Impact:

27. Device: *polysyndeton*
    Impact:

28. Device: *anaphora*
    Impact:

29. Device: *parallelism/anaphora*
    Impact:

30. Device: *parallelism*
    Impact:

Dramatically Improve Student Writing
with our Powerful New Writing Program!

3 Simple Truths and 6 Essential Traits of Powerful Writing™

- Improve student test scores
- Unify your school's writing curriculum
- Provide clear goals for your students
- Track development across grade levels
- Build a clear process for monitoring student progress
- Make the abstract process of grading writing more concrete

Once you've seen how students can develop from novice writers to proficient, powerful writers through our highly organized system, you'll wonder how you ever taught writing before.

In developing this program, we've focused on the needs of today's teachers. *3 Simple Truths and 6 Essential Traits of Powerful Writing,*™ provides teachers with a clear framework for teaching and evaluating writing, including a starting and ending point for each grade, a wide variety of writing prompts and exercises, and concrete guidelines for the difficult job of grading subjective essays.

The clarity of objectives provided by the unique 14-point rubric will help your students fully understand not only their current status, but also what they need to do in order to improve.

No Risk Guarantee!

We guarantee that you've never seen a more effective writing program—and we'll prove it with this unprecedented guarantee. Buy a class set of books with the accompanying CD for $240.00; then, use the program for an entire year. If you don't agree that it's the best program available, return the battered, bruised, soiled, and marked material, and we'll refund your purchase price of $240.00, plus shipping. *There's nothing to lose!*

Introductory Price!

Book I: Novice Level
301633	Class Set of 30 Books and CD Teacher's Guide	~~$299.99~~	$240.00
301612	Single Copy	~~$10.95~~	$8.95

Book II: Developing Level
301634	Class Set of 30 Books and CD Teacher's Guide	~~$299.99~~	$240.00
301613	Single Copy	~~$10.95~~	$8.95

Book III: Advancing Level
301635	Class Set of 30 Books and CD Teacher's Guide	~~$299.99~~	$240.00
301614	Single Copy	~~$10.95~~	$8.95

Book IV: Proficient Level
301636	Class Set of 30 Books and CD Teacher's Guide	~~$299.99~~	$240.00
301615	Single Copy	~~$10.95~~	$8.95

Prestwick House

Call toll free: (800)932-4593   Fax 24/7: (888)718-9333

Visit us online at **www.prestwickhouse.com**